NEW ENGLAND'S PROSPECT

William Wood   ✕   Edited by Alden T. Vaughan

The Commonwealth Series   *Winfred E. A. Bernhard, General Editor*

University of Massachusetts Press ✒ Amherst, 1977

The title page and map from
William Wood, *New England's Prospect* (London, 1634)
are reproduced by permission of
The Houghton Library, Harvard University

To Alden Gibson Vaughan
Classical Scholar
and
Peripatetic New Englander

Contents

Series Editor's Preface

William Wood's *New England's Prospect,* briskly written, pleasantly informative and interspersed with wit, stands out among the accounts of early New England. Responding to widespread English curiosity about the New England scene, Wood presented his book, as the original title page indicates, to "both enrich the knowledge of the mind-travelling Reader, or benefit the future Voyager." His work, brief as it was, became one of the earliest published sources describing lucidly the area of the Massachusetts Bay Colony.

Alden Vaughan, professor of Colonial American history at Columbia University, has produced a new, scholarly edition of this rare work. Through his careful editing, Professor Vaughan has retrieved *New England's Prospect* from undeserved obscurity. Striking a judicious balance in his approach to editing, he has retained Wood's rich, colorful words, as well as the vigor and flavor of his style. Yet he has modernized the text sufficiently to eliminate the impediments to the modern reader which are frequently evident in seventeenth-century prose.

This presentation of Wood's analytical essay is an important addition to the Commonwealth Series. The first two volumes, *God's Plot* and *Letters from New England,* involve various facets of the lives of the first generation of Puritan settlers in Massachusetts. Professor Michael McGiffert edited the autobiography and journal of the well-known Reverend Thomas Shepard, which had not been previously published in entirety.

Ably presenting these unusual documents, he has guided the reader into the intricacies of the Puritan mind in its restless quest for the assurance of salvation. In *Letters from New England,* Professor Everett Emerson brought together all extant correspondence from the Puritan newcomers in Massachusetts Bay Colony to their countrymen in England. This collection graphically reveals the hazards of oceanic voyage and first settlement for these transplanted Englishmen. The volumes in the Series are fresh editions of historical materials of permanent significance relating to the evolution of New England as a whole. In each book the text of the original is set in historical context by an authoritative introduction.

As a work of history *New England's Prospect* has continuing significance in revealing the early interaction of the white man with the New England environment. More extensive in its treatment than the Reverend Francis Higginson's contemporary *New-Englands Plantation,* Wood's account is also far more imaginative in depicting the distinctive fauna and flora which came to the attention of the English observer. Even more interesting for the modern "mind-travelling Reader" than the Reverend Higginson's comments on the native Indians is William Wood's sympathetic portrayal of the coastal Indians' way of life. At times sophisticated in his observations, at times revealing a naive sense of wonder about the New World, the author, nevertheless, makes vividly clear the intense impact that the land and its inhabitants had on the earliest settlers.

Winfred E. A. Bernhard

Amherst, Massachusetts
February 1977

Introduction

Seventeenth-century England craved news of America. As British out-
posts sprouted along the Atlantic seaboard—at Jamestown, Plymouth,
Massachusetts Bay, Maryland—Englishmen read avidly the reports sent
home by explorers and colonists. Some of the literature about America
was intentionally inaccurate, and much of it was unintentionally misleading, but as the quantity mounted a few items of superior quality
emerged. From those careful writings the English public gradually acquired a realistic sense of what America was and what it might become.
By the end of the 1620s readers knew from several publications about
the great tribulations and even greater potential of early Virginia and
Plymouth; in the early 1630s English attention shifted to Massachusetts
Bay where thousands of colonists, largely inspired by Puritan theology,
had begun a remarkable new experiment in overseas colonization. Almost everyone, whether friend or foe of the experiment, or merely curious onlooker, awaited the reports that brought news and advice. But
until 1634 there was no single book to which prospective colonists and
others could turn for reliable information about England's latest American venture.[1]

1. Several publications before 1634 gave readers a glimpse of New England's geography and native inhabitants, though none had Wood's thoroughness or singleness
of purpose. Among the best were John Brereton, *Briefe and True Relation of the*

That year London bookseller John Bellamie offered a slender new volume for sale at his Three Golden Lions shop in Cornhill. William Wood's *New England's Prospect* promised its readers—as its prolix subtitle boasted—*A true, lively, and experimental description of that part of America, commonly called New England: discovering the state of that country, both as it stands to our new-come English planters; and to the old native inhabitants, laying down that which may both enrich the knowledge of the mind-traveling reader or benefit the future voyager.* The author had recently returned from four years in Massachusetts and wanted to share his excitement and knowledge of the New World.

Wood's claim to be "true, lively, and experimental" did not mislead. His book was unusually accurate among the swelling literature on British America; it was relatively lucid in an era of turgid prose; and it was truly "experimental" in the sense Wood intended and his readers understood, that is, based on experience. And it was, as the subtitle proclaimed, primarily a "description"—not a history, not a chronicle of events, not an argumentative tract—of the region inhabited by "our new-come English planters" and their Indian neighbors. The first part of the book explained New England's geography and biology: the coastline, climate, soil, and flora and fauna of Massachusetts (which Wood and most of his contemporaries considered synonymous with New England). Only the final three chapters of Part One focused on settlement: one offered a brief account of the Massachusetts towns that existed when Wood left New England in the summer of 1633; another discussed "the evils, and such things as are hurtful in the plantation" (principally wolves, rattlesnakes, and mosquitoes) and how to thwart them; while the final chapter in Part One advised prospective colonists how to prepare for the voyage and first year of settlement. Part Two described the Indians of New England, including a brief assessment of each major tribe, generalizations on Indian customs and qualities—their appearance, food, temperament, government, marriage customs, religion, recreation,

---

Discoverie of the North Part of Virginia (1602); James Rosier, *A True Relation of the Voyage of Captaine George Waymouth* (1605); John Smith, *A Description of New England* (1616); William Morell, *New England, or a Briefe Narration* (1625); Christopher Levett, *A Voyage into New England* (1628); and Francis Higginson, *New England's Plantation, or a Short and True Description of the Commodities and Discommodities of the Country* (1630).

and much more. *New England's Prospect* closed with a five page vocabulary of Indian words and phrases from which, Wood hoped, readers might "reap delight, if they can get no profit."[2]

New England's Prospect sold well enough to justify a second edition the following year. It varied only slightly from the original: Wood took the opportunity to correct some printer's errors and to insert a few marginal notes, and he made some minor alterations based on new information. A third edition, in 1639, followed almost verbatim the text of the second. Three separate editions in five years, each entirely reset except for the large frontispiece map (which varied in its caption but not in its cartography), testified to the extraordinary interest Wood's account aroused among English readers.

Wood's fellow writers had high regard for the book. "He that desyres to know more of the Estate of new England," advised Judocus Hondy's *Historia Mundi or Mercator's Atlas,* "lett him read a Book of the prospecte of new England & ther he shall have satisfaction."[3] That same year (1635) an anonymous pamphlet promoting the colonization of Maryland urged readers with "a Curiosity to know all that hath beene observed of the customes and manners of the Indians" to consult Captain John Smith's writings on Virginia "and Mr. Woods of New-England."[4] Two years later Thomas Morton's *New English Canaan* made frequent and usually favorable references to the work of "my countryman Mr. Wood," though Morton's irrepressible wit caused him, in several instances, to cite "that wodden prospect."[5]

I

Despite *New England's Prospect*'s several editions and abundant merit, little is known about its author. Wood mentioned in his preface that he spent four years in Massachusetts, and he noted elsewhere that he had

2. See below, pp. 117–24.
3. Quoted in the Prince Society edition of Wood's *New England's Prospect* (Boston, 1865), p. viii.
4. "A Relation of Maryland," in Clayton Coleman Hall, ed., *Narratives of Early Maryland, 1633–1684* (New York, 1910), p. 83.
5. Thomas Morton, *New English Canaan* (Amsterdam, 1637; repr. New York, 1972), pp. 27, 28, 38, 53, 84.

returned to England in August of 1633.[6] Those are his only autobiographical passages. A few other scraps of information appear in the records of the Massachusetts Bay colony: in 1631 a "William Woods," presumably the author, took the Freeman's Oath along with 115 other settlers,[7] and in September 1634 the General Court of Massachusetts ordered that "lettres of thankefullnes [be] signed by the Court, and sent to the Countesse of Warwicke, Mr. Paynter, Mr. Wood, and others, that have been benefactors to this plantation."[8] This was almost certainly a recognition of New England's Prospect's recent publication.

Everything else that can be said about William Wood is conjectural. Nothing is known of his date or place of birth, or of his upbringing; his style, howev r, suggests that English was his native tongue and that he received some formal education. But he cannot be distinguished from the innumerable William Woods who appear in the records of Stuart England. Nothing therefore can be said about his occupation or family background, although the absence of "Mr." before his name in the 1631 list of freemen implies that he was not of the gentry class. The addition of an honorific "Mr." in the 1634 entry probably reflects the colony's gratitude rather than a rise in status.

A few speculations about Wood seem plausible though undocumented. Assuming that he reached New England in the summer of 1629 (i.e., four years before his departure in 1633), he must have been among the small group that settled in Salem under John Endecott a year before Governor John Winthrop arrived with more than a thousand followers and the royal charter to mark the formal beginning of the Bay Colony. Wood's residence in New England before the bulk of the settlers came may partly account for his emphasis on flora, fauna, and the native inhabitants, and for his scant attention to the English colonists. Wood's early arrival may also explain his return to England in 1633. The Endecott group was, on the whole, a scouting party; its members were not necessarily committed to Puritan beliefs nor to the creation of a Puritan state. Wood's departure in 1633, combined with the relatively secular

6. See below pp. 20 and 65. Wood probably sailed on the *Elizabeth Bonaventure* which left Boston on August 15, the date Wood gives for his departure.
7. Nathaniel B. Shurtleff, ed., *Records of the Governor and Company of the Massachusetts Bay in New England (1628–86)* (5 vols.; Boston, 1853–54), 1, 366.
8. Ibid., p. 128.

tone of his writing, suggests that he may have been a New Englander but not a Puritan.[9] *New England's Prospect* is uncommonly free of the religious rhetoric that infused early New England prose.

Also conjectural, but also based on clues in *New England's Prospect,* are where and when Wood wrote his book. Because he always referred to New England as *there,* never as *here,* Wood probably composed it upon his return to England. However, in the nineteenth century a tantalizing version of the book's origin appeared in the "diary" of Obediah Turner, an early settler of Saugus (later Lynn), where Wood may have lived before his departure. One evening in 1633, Turner claimed,

> I did have much pleasant discourse with William Woode . . . while sitting on the oak logg by my back doore; for he hath given oute that he shall presentlie depart for Old England, there to sojourn a briefe space. He hath bin here from the beginning of the settlement, and hath writ enow to make a faire booke, aboute affaires within the pattent. And I did mch urge him to printe the booke while in England. He hath trauelled mch amongst the settlements and by chearfull wordes and other wise helpes stopped manie that would haue gon from vs, some to Virginia, some to Plymouth and some elsewhere. And the book, mch of wch he hath read to me, speaking to our praise and to the praise of the land, I doubt not, being printed at home, will doe greatlie for vs, as there be manie who want but to be shure of our being well planted firste and they will send over mch to our comforte and helpe. But some things he hath putt down that methinks will not looke well in printe and I would faine haue had him drop them; as his discourse about lions at Cape Anne. Quoth I, I doe not beleave that anie such beaste ever was founde there. He, being a little heady, did warmly replie, that then they were Devills, for nothing but one or the other could make such terrible roareings as have been hearde thereaboute. And soe, said he, I will have it one or the other. Well,

9. On pre-1630 settlement in Massachusetts see Samuel Eliot Morison, *Builders of the Bay Colony* (Boston, 1930), chs. 1-2. Wood and many others who preceded the Great Migration became freemen before the Court decreed that only church members could qualify. See ibid., p. 85. Cf. Charles Edward Banks, *The Winthrop Fleet of 1630* (Boston, 1930), p. 98, which lists the "William Woods" who became a freeman in 1631 among the passengers arriving in the summer of 1630.

well, quoth I, Master Woode, if so you will, it must be, tho I would faine haue all discourse about revenous beastes and Devills left out. If it be thot at home that our lande doth abounde in such, but few will be founde readie to come hither. Lions they cannot be for the bookes of trauell have it that such beastes live onlie in burning desert lands. Devills they may be, for such be found everiewhere. And as manie would rather face Devills than lions, it were better to call them Devills if one or the other it must be. And blessed be God wee have the holie Bible for protection against them.[10]

It is tempting to think that such a conversation took place and that Wood had completed his manuscript while still in America. But the episode and the "diary" were only figments of the imagination of James Robinson Newhall, or "Obediah Redpath" as his pseudonym proclaimed, who clothed his history of early Lynn in the style of Washington Irving's "Father Knickerbocker."

Most conjectural of all is Wood's subsequent career. The additions to the second edition imply that he was still in England in 1635. Then he slips into obscurity. Late in 1635 a William Wood sailed into Massachusetts Bay aboard *Hopewell.* His age was listed as 27, his occupation as "husbandman."[11] This may have been the author of *New England's Prospect,* but if so, the surviving records are strangely silent about the return of a man who had brought the colony so much favorable publicity. Neither the colonial records nor Governor Winthrop and the other early chroniclers mentioned the newly arrived Wood as the author of *New England's Prospect.* The Wood who came in 1635 lived first at Saugus and represented that town in the General Court of 1636. In 1637 a William Wood helped to found Sandwich, and a William Wood died in Concord in 1670 or 1671. But there is no evidence by which to link this man—or men—to *New England's Prospect.*[12]

10. [James Robinson Newhall], *Lin: or Jewels of the Third Plantation* (Lynn, Mass., 1862), pp. 62f.
11. Alonzo Lewis, *The History of Lynn, Including Nahant* (2 ed., Boston, 1844), pp. 61f.
12. James Savage, *A Genealogical Dictionary of the First Settlers of New England* (4 vols.; Boston, 1860–1862), 4, 630; Allen Johnson and Dumas Malone, eds., *Dictionary of American Biography* (New York, 1928–), 20, 476.

II

The lasting value of *New England's Prospect* is threefold: as natural history, as ethnology, and as an example of early American descriptive literature. In all three categories, Wood was in some ways deficient. Because he was not a scientist, his observations on flora and fauna are often imprecise; because he spent little time with the Indians (he does not say how much personal contact he had, but clearly it was limited), his account of Indian life is sometimes unreliable; because he was not a gifted writer, his prose is occasionally obtuse and frequently awkward. But his flaws are relatively minor. As a natural historian, ethnologist, and descriptive writer William Wood made major contributions to the literature of early New England.

Seventeenth-century visitors to the New World were fascinated by its natural wonders. Their interest stemmed partly from the practical need to find commodities that could be exported: colonies were supposed to be self-supporting and their backers expected to reap a profit. Hence the early explorers and settlers whose writings survive were, almost without exception, deeply concerned with the commercial opportunities afforded by America. Equally prevalent in New World reporting was the excitement of finding a land that bore some resemblance to the homeland as well as some remarkable differences. But most early American authors let their information about the plants and animals of the New World take second seat to their other interests—historical in John Smith's case, satirical in Thomas Morton's, theological in Roger Williams's.[13] In the eighteenth century skilled scientific observers would record in precise detail America's plant and animal life; the seventeenth century had to rely for its biological data on untrained reporters who crammed, often awkwardly, a bit of natural history into works of different intent.

William Wood was an exception. In marked contrast to most other early New England writers, he focused directly on the land and its vegetation, and on its human and animal inhabitants. He wrote nothing about

13. See Edward Arber and A. G. Bradley, eds., *Travels and Works of Captain John Smith* (2 vols.; Edinburgh, 1910); Morton, *New English Canaan*; and James Hammond Trumbull *et al.,* eds., *The Complete Writings of Roger Williams* (7 vols.; New York, 1963).

the history of the Puritan movement, the setting up of churches, the creation of governments, or the struggle for religious and social purity. Much, to be sure, can be learned from a close reading of *New England's Prospect* about the problems of English life in America—the difficulty of clearing the ground, the paucity of draft animals (leading some settlers to contemplate harnessing the moose), the shortage of beer, the need for interpreters, and other insights into mundane aspects of colonization. But these are incidental to Wood's purpose. He devotes whole paragraphs, many of them lengthy, to clams, cherries, otters and mosquitoes; entire chapters to birds, fish, and forest animals. Wood thus produced the earliest comprehensive record of New England's natural resources at the beginning of European settlement. Gradually other works—especially Thomas Morton's in 1637 and John Josselyn's in 1672—corrected and expanded Wood's information.[14] His, however, was the point of departure, the base from which later accounts had to advance.

New England's Prospect is even more valuable as ethnology than as biology. Wood spent little time among the Indians—compared, for instance, to New England's Roger Williams or John Eliot or Daniel Gookin. And Wood probably had little experience with other non-English cultures—compared to Virginia's Captain John Smith or William Strachey—against which to measure Indian society. But Wood's curiosity and thoroughness largely compensated for his limitations. He appears to have assiduously collected information from other settlers to augment his own observations, and he presents his findings with refreshingly little of the cultural ethnocentricity so common to seventeenth-century Englishmen. Especially appealing is the range of his description. Like most European portrayals of the Indians, Wood's treats their appearance, government, religion, and warfare. He is unique, however, in giving almost equal attention to Indian daily life: how they gambled, played football, and practiced archery. He expounds too on Indian diet, hunting and fishing techniques, the role of women in Indian society, and on variations within the New England Algonquian languages. And

14. See Morton, *New English Canaan*; John Josselyn, *New England's Rarities Discovered* (London, 1672; repr. American Antiquarian Society, *Transactions and Collections*, 4 [1860]); and John Josselyn, *An Account of Two Voyages to New-England* (London, 1675; repr. Massachusetts Historical Society, *Collections*, 3rd. ser. 3 [1833]).

because he viewed the tribes before English expansion caused major dis-
integration and migration, Wood's delineation of the principal tribal ter-
ritories and characteristics is a major contribution to understanding the
numbers and distribution of the New England Indians at the time of
European contact. Not everything Wood wrote about the Indians is cor-
roborated by other observers or by modern anthropological evidence.
But in his ethnological chapters, as in those on botany and zoology,
Wood remains a basic and generally reliable source.

Some of the interest in *New England's Prospect* stems from its literary characteristics. As one of the earliest American writers, he foreshad-
owed an emergent literary tradition. Like John Smith, William Bradford,
and other early chroniclers, Wood represented the first stage of that tradition—authors who wrote on American topics from an English background and in an English idiom.

Seventeenth-century writers often tried to impress their readers with
quotations from several languages, with classical allusions, and with
complex syntax. Whatever their effect on the authors' contemporaries,
such devices seem stultifying to modern readers. William Wood is a welcome contrast. He could not avoid all of the stylistic conventions of his
day—especially in the cumbersome and deferential dedication to Sir William Armyne. But he came close; he uses only occasional Latin phrases
and has few references to ancient authors and events. On the whole, he
is crisp, succinct, and direct. As Moses Coit Tyler noted in his influential
study of early American literature, Wood "attained the fine art of pack-
ing his pages full of the most exact delineation of facts, without pressing
the life and juice out of them; and, besides the extraordinary raciness
and vivacity of his manner, he has an elegance of touch by no means
common in . . . his contemporaries."[15] No dry sermonizer, Wood es-
chewed the moralistic tone of so much of his era's prose. His book is
accordingly both informative and enjoyable.

Wood's felicitous style was no accident. He clearly tried to please his
readers through imaginative and sometimes humorous metaphors and by
inserting occasional passages of verse. Four fairly lengthy poetic descriptions of trees, land animals, birds, and fish supplement the prose passages. These are not entirely successful as poetry, but they are better

15. *A History of American Literature, 1607-1765* (2 vols., New York, 1878; repr.
in 1 vol., New York, 1962), p. 166.

than the works many of his contemporaries produced—better by far than the awkward efforts of such fellow New Englanders as William Bradford and William Morrell. Wood's verse essay on trees (here produced exactly as in the 1635 edition) is representative:

> Trees both in hills and plaines, in plenty be,
> The long liv'd Oake, and mournefull Cypris tree,
> Skie towring pines, and Chesnuts coated rough,
> The lasting Cedar, with the Walnut tough:
> The rozin dropping Firre for masts in use,
> The Boatmen seeke for Oares light, neate, growne sprewse,
> The brittle Ash, the ever trembling Aspes,
> The broad-spread Elme, whose concave harbours waspes,
> The water spungie Alder good for nought,
> Small Elderne by th'*Indian* Fletchers sought,
> The knottie Maple, pallid Birtch, Hawthornes,
> The Horne bound tree that to be cloven scornes;
> Which from the tender Vine oft take his spouse,
> Who twinds imbracing armes about his boughes. . . .[16]

Wood's poetry avoids being commonplace because it fits his major purpose—to inform as well as to entertain. It is not simply an arboreal list; by telling much about the use of trees in New England it becomes an integral part of the text rather than a rhetorical flourish.

Wood's humor served as another device to blend information with enjoyment. He admitted in his preface "To the Reader," that the section on Indians had been written in a "light and facetious style"; he had "inserted many passages of mirth concerning them to spice the rest of my more serious discourse and to make it more pleasant."[17] But the section on flora and fauna contains as many attempts to amuse the reader. Even the climate can be treated humorously: the northwest wind, Wood warned, commands "every man to his house, forbidding any to outface him without prejudice to their noses."[18] Wood's lightheartedness must have been welcome in an era of ponderous prose.

Some of Wood's humor is directed at aspects of New England that had received unfavorable attention and was thus a subtle way of diminishing

16. See below, p. 39.
17. See below, p. 20.
18. See below, p. 28.

criticism of the region. Such a tactic nicely served another of Wood's purposes: enticing other Englishmen to America. For *New England's Prospect* was not merely description; it was also promotional literature and as such belongs among the best examples of that genre. Wood was far less bombastic than many of the other publicists of colonization, was more willing to present a balanced view, and was less aggressive in his solicitations. But his intent is clear. He admits in his preface that he will refute "many scandalous and false reports" about the colony, and throughout the book he stresses New England's virtues while minimizing its faults. He glosses over the hazards of early settlement (such as its high mortality and widespread suffering), ignores some conditions altogether (religious controversy, for example), and puts the best face possible on the weather, the soil, and the availability of food. Few readers could have missed Wood's point: that New England offered unparalleled opportunities, and the few hardships and dangers could be avoided by following the author's sage advice.

To some extent Wood's promotional rhetoric reflected the effort at self-justification that underlay much early American writing. Like many other chroniclers, Wood seized the chance to justify the bold move he himself had made, probably in the face of warnings from friends and relatives. By 1634 Massachusetts had emerged as Britain's most successful experiment in colonization; whether Wood intended to return there (as he proclaimed) or not, he could boast a bit of the natural wonders and the prospects for further settlement that he had witnessed. *New England's Prospect* bore a touch of self-congratulation.

III

Three editions of *New England's Prospect* have appeared since the London editions of the 1630s, all in America. None is based on Wood's corrected version of 1635, and only one is accurately transcribed. All retain Wood's confusing syntax, punctuation, and spelling.

The first American edition was published in 1764 when an anonymous editor—subsequently identified with reasonable surety as Nathaniel Rogers of Boston—reprinted the 1639 version.[19] Apparently unaware of the 1635 publication, Rogers erred in identifying his as the third edition.

---

19. Massachusetts Historical Society, *Proceedings,* 6 (1862–1863), 250f., 334–337.

He also unwisely substituted for Wood's prefatory material a long essay of his own; and he, or someone else, also added several lengthy annotations to the text. The new material did little to improve the book. Instead it reflects the interests and biases of its time. The introduction barely mentions Wood but dwells on the role of the colonies within the British Empire and the dangers of arbitrary government, while the annotations to Wood's text present a hodge-podge of opinions, including some that were highly derogatory toward the Indians. Wood had portrayed the American natives quite favorably; the 1764 edition grumbled about "their immense sloth, their incapacity to consider abstract truth . . . and their perpetual wanderings, which prevent a steady worship. . . . The feroce manners of a native Indian," it concluded, "can never be effaced, nor can the most finished politeness totally eradicate the wild lines of his education."[20]

Two editions of *New England's Prospect* appeared in the nineteenth century. In 1865 the Prince Society reissued the 1634 version as part of its series of early Americana. This edition adhered with commendable accuracy to Wood's original, deviating from it only to correct the printer's errors and to add a brief preface by Charles Deane, a specialist on early New England. It also reprinted Nathaniel Rogers' curious introduction to the 1764 edition, though fortunately not his annotations.

The Prince Society issued only 170 copies, and *New England's Prospect* soon became inaccessible. In 1898 Eben Moody Boynton of West Newbury, Massachusetts, a descendant of Wood who lamented the scarcity of his ancestor's book, issued still another edition. It followed the Prince Society version for the most part but substituted an introduction by Boynton for those of Deane and Rogers. It also changed most of the italicized words to Roman type and made minor alterations in spelling, capitalization, and punctuation, and dispensed with the long "s" of all previous editions. Unfortunately, Boynton's introduction was uninformative and infelicitous, and his transcription of the text was frequently inaccurate. And the 1898 edition, like its predecessors, has long been out-of-print.

Despite the vagaries of the several editions, Wood's *New England's Prospect* has been used extensively by scholars in many disciplines, and

20. Roger's preface is most readily consulted in the Prince Society edition of *New England's Prospect.* The quotations are from the 1764 edition, p. 94.

portions of it have appeared in anthologies of early American writings. But the absence of a modern edition has prevented Wood's classic from reaching the audience it deserves and has forced scholars to use inconvenient or unreliable versions. The Commonwealth edition seeks to remedy the situation by presenting a version that remains faithful to Wood's words while improving the typography of his presentation.

EDITORIAL CRITERIA

The Commonwealth edition of *New England's Prospect* is based on Wood's second edition (1635) on the assumption that it, rather than the first edition, was the author's most complete and accurate text. If Wood did not return to Massachusetts in 1635, he may have been in London when the 1639 version appeared; if so he made no significant changes in his account, despite the Bay Colony's considerable growth in the intervening years. The third edition must therefore be considered merely a reissue of the second and probably was printed without the author's assistance. However, the map that accompanied the first edition is reproduced here because no changes were incorporated in subsequent editions.

I have introduced several modifications in the text of the present edition in order to make Wood's observations more readable and informative. In keeping with modern editorial procedure, I have applied today's standards of spelling, italicizing, capitalization, punctuation, and abbreviation. I have also broken up excessively long sentences where appropriate and have divided his almost endless paragraphs into more manageable portions. The words, however, remain Wood's. None have been deleted, except a few place-names in the margins that merely indicated the contents of adjacent paragraphs. No words have been added, except a few in square brackets to clarify Wood's meaning. And no words have been changed in content: the orthography is modern, but the lexicon conforms exactly to Wood's intentions. For example, his *"Indian* Corne" becomes "Indian corn"; his "ships, and houses, & Mils" becomes "ships and houses and mills." But "hath," "pompion," and "milch" are retained as Wood wrote them because they were *bona fide* words in his day. Their obsolescence does not justify changing them to "has," "pumpkin," and "milk" without undermining the integrity of Wood's text. In sum, if the present edition were read aloud, it would *sound* the same as the edition of 1635. The reader, however, would not have to struggle with Wood's confusing capitalization, stumble over his idiosyncratic spelling and punctuation, or cope with his erratic use of italics and his meandering syntax. Shorn of its seventeenth-century typographical oddities, Wood's message should come through more clearly and enjoyably.

Three kinds of annotations appear in the footnotes. First, I have attempted to identify, whenever possible, the people and places mentioned by Wood. Second, I have defined words and phrases that are not usually found in single-volume dictionaries but have not provided definitions of terms such as pipkin, killick, froe, and calenture because, however rare, they are in such dictionaries. Third, I have occasionally cited authoritative works, both seventeenth-century sources and recent monographs, that shed further light on Wood's text. Such annotation is merely suggestive; a thorough documentation of Wood's observations would require a separate volume and would exceed the intentions of the Commonwealth Series. Instead, the annotations have the same goal as the modernization of the text: to make *New England's Prospect* serviceable to the modern reader.

ACKNOWLEDGMENTS

I am grateful to the Houghton Library of Harvard University and to the New-York Historical Society for access to their copies of the several editions of *New England's Prospect*. Harvard's Charles Warren Center provided essential financial and clerical support during the early stages of this edition; Columbia University's William A. Dunning Fund helped with the final stage. I am deeply indebted to both universities.

I have also received important assistance from Barry W. Bienstock, who helped to prepare the annotations and to verify the text of this edition, and from Alden Gibson Vaughan, who translated the Latin phrases. My thanks to them and to others—librarians, typists, colleagues, and friends—who generously gave their time and talent.

NEVV ENGLANDS PROSPECT.

A true, lively, and experimen-
tall description of that part of *America*,
commonly called NEVV ENGLAND:
discovering the state of that Coun-
trie, both as it stands to our new-come
English Planters; and to the old
Native Inhabitants.

Laying downe that which may both enrich the
knowledge of the mind-travelling Reader,
or benefit the future Voyager.

By WILLIAM WOOD.

Printed at *London* by *Tho. Cotes*, for *Iohn Bellamie*, and are to be sold
at his shop, at the three Golden Lyons in *Corne-hill*, neere the
Royall Exchange. 1634.

The South part of Nevv-England, as it is Planted this yeare, 1634.

To the Right Worshipful,
my much honored friend,
Sir William Armyne,
Knight and Baronet.[1]

Noble Sir,

The good assurance of your native worth, and thrice generous disposition, as also the continual manifestation of your bounteous favor and love towards myself in particular, hath so bound my thankful acknowledgment that I count it the least part of my service to present the first fruits of my far-fetched experience to the kind acceptance of your charitable hands.

Well knowing that though this, my work, own[s] not worth enough to deserve your patronage,[2] yet such is your benign humanity that I am confident you will deign it your protection, under which it willingly shrouds itself. And as it is reported of that man whose name was Alexander, being a cowardly milksop by nature, yet hearing of the valiant courage of that magnificent hero, Alexander the Great, whose name he bore, he thenceforth became stout and valorous; and as he was animated by hav-

1. Sir William Armyne (1593–1651; sometimes spelled Armine) of Osgoodby, Lincolnshire, was a member of Parliament in the 1620s and 1640s, sheriff of Lincolnshire in the 1630s, and later in the Council of State. The nature of Wood's connection with Sir William and of Sir William's interest in New England have not been established, but the first paragraph of the dedication strongly suggests that Armyne subsidized *New England's Prospect*. And in keeping with the deferential customs of that era, Wood's gratitude is couched in florid and convoluted prose—in marked contrast to the rest of his book.
2. This acknowledgment of Arymne's largess appears in all three seventeenth-century editions, although financial support was probably needed only for the first.

ing the very name of puissant Aléxander, so shall these my weak and feeble labors receive life and courage by the patronage of your much esteemed self, whereby they shall be able to outface the keenest fangs of a black-mouthed Momus.[3] For from hence the world may conclude that either there was some worth in the book that caused so wise a person to look upon it and to vouchsafe to own it, or else if they suppose that in charity he fostered it, as being a poor helpless brat, they may thence learn to do so likewise.

If here I should take upon me the usual strain of a soothing epistolizer, I should (though upon better grounds than many) sound forth a full-mouthed encomiastic of your incomparable worth; but though your deserts may justly challenge it, yet I know your virtuous modesty would not thank me for it. And indeed, your own actions are the best heralds of your own praise, which in spite of envy itself must speak you wise and truly noble. And I for my part, if I may but present anything which either for its profit or delight may obtain your favorable approbation, I have already reaped the harvest of my expectation. Only I must desire you to pardon my bold presumption as thus to make your well-deserving name the frontispiece to so rude and ill-deserving frame. Thus wishing a confluence of all blessings both of the throne and footstool to be multiplied upon yourself and your virtuous consort, my very good lady, together with all the stems of your noble family, I take my leave and rest,

Your Worship's to serve
and be commanded,
W. W.

3. From Greek mythology; a carping critic.

To the Reader

Courteous Reader:

Though I will promise thee no such voluptuous discourse as many have made upon a scanter subject (though they have travailed[4] no further than the smoke of their own native chimneys) yet dare I presume to present thee with the true and faithful relation of some few years travels and experience, wherein I would be loath to broach anything which may puzzle thy belief, and so justly draw upon myself that unjust aspersion commonly laid on travelers, of whom many say, "They may lie by authority because none can control them." Which proverb had surely his original from the sleepy belief of many a home-bred dormouse who comprehends not either the rarity or possibility of those things he sees not, to whom the most classic relations seem riddles and paradoxes, of whom it may be said, as once of Diogenes, that because he circled himself in the circumference of a tub, he therefore contemned the port and palace of Alexander which he knew not. So there are many a tub-brained cynic who because anything stranger than ordinary is too large for the straight hoops of his apprehension, he preemptorily concludes it is a lie.

But I decline this sort of thick-witted readers, and dedicate the mite

4. "Travail" and "travel" were originally the same word. By the seventeenth century the former usually carried its present connotation of "toil," while "travel" applied to journeys. But usage was inconsistent. In using "travail" here and elsewhere, Wood may have intended to emphasize the difficulty of travel to and in America—i.e., his travels were unusually toilsome.

of my endeavors to my more credulous, ingenious, and less censorious countrymen, for whose sakes I undertook this work; and I did it the rather because there hath some relations heretofore past the press which have been very imperfect, as also because there hath been many scandalous and false reports past upon the country, even from the sulphurious breath of every base ballad-monger. Wherefore to perfect the one and take off the other, I have laid down the nature of the country, without any partial respect unto it, as being my dwelling place where I have lived these four years and intend, God willing, to return shortly again. But my conscience is to me a thousand witnesses that what I speak is the very truth, and this will inform thee almost as fully concerning it as if thou wentest over to see it. Now whereas I have written the latter part of this relation concerning the Indians in a more light and facetious style than the former, because their carriage and behavior hath afforded more matter of mirth and laughter than gravity and wisdom, and therefore I have inserted many passages of mirth concerning them to spice the rest of my more serious discourse and to make it more pleasant. Thus thou mayest in two or three hours travail over a few leaves see and know that which cost him that writ it years and travail over sea and land before he knew it. And therefore I hope thou wilt accept it, which shall be my full reward as it was my whole ambition, and so I rest,

Thine bound in what I may,
W. W.

To the Author, his singular good
friend, Mr. William Wood

Thanks to thy travel and thyself, who hast
Much knowledge in so small room, comptly[5] placed.
And thine experience thus a mount dost make,
From whence we may *New England's Prospect* take,
Though many thousands distant, wherefore thou
Thyself shalt sit upon Mount Praise her brow.
For if the man that shall the short cut find
Unto the Indies, shall for that be shrined,
Sure thou deservest then no small praise, who,
So short cut to New England here dost show.
And if than this small thanks thou gettest no more,
Of thanks I then will say the world's grown poor.

S. W.[6]

5. I.e., elegantly.
6. The author of this poem has not been identified.

The Table

[Part One]

CHAP. 1

Of the Situation, Bays, Havens, and Inlets

For as much as the king's most excellent majesty hath been graciously pleased, by the grant of his letters patents, at first to give life to the plantations of New England and hath daily likewise by his favors and royal protection cherished their growing hopes, whereby many of his majesty's faithful subjects have been imboldened to venture persons, states, and endeavors to the enlargement of his dominions in that western continent; wherefore I thought fit (for the further encouragement of those that hereafter, either by purse or person, shall help forward the plantation) to set forth these few observations out of my personal and experimental knowledge.

The place whereon the English have built their colonies is judged by those who have best skill in discovery either to be an island, surrounded on the north side with the spacious River Canada and on the south with Hudson's River, or else a peninsula, these two rivers overlapping one another, having their rise from the great lakes which are not far off one another, as the Indians do certainly inform us. But it is not my intent to wander far from our patent; wherefore I refer you to the thrice memorable discoverer of those parts, Captain Smith, who hath likewise fully described the southern and northeast part of New England, with the noted headlands, capes, harbors, rivers, ponds, and lakes, with the nature of the soil, and commodities both by sea and land, etc., within the degrees of forty-one and forty-five.[1]

The bay of Massachusetts lieth under the degree of forty-two and forty-three, bearing southwest from the Land's End of England, at the bottom whereof are situated most of the English plantations. This bay is both safe, spacious, and deep, free from such cockling seas as run upon the coast of Ireland and in the channels of England. There be no stiff running currents or rocks, shelves, bars, quicksands. The mariners, having sailed two or three leagues towards the bottom, may behold the two capes embracing their welcome ships in their arms, which thrust themselves out into the sea in form of a half-moon, the surrounding shore being high and showing many white cliffs in a most pleasant prospect, with diverse places of low land out of which diverse rivers vent themselves into the ocean, with many openings where is good harboring for ships of any burthen; so that if an unexpected storm or crosswind should bar the mariner from recovering his desired port, he may reach other harbors, as Plymouth, Cape Ann, Salem, Marvill Head [i.e., Marblehead]; all of which afford good ground for anchorage, being likewise landlocked from wind and seas. The chief and usual harbor is the still bay of Massachusetts, which is close aboard the plantations, in which most of our ships come to anchor, being the nearest their mart and usual place of landing of passengers. It is a safe and pleasant harbor within, having but one common and safe entrance, and that not very broad, there scarce being room for three ships to come inboard and board at a time. But being once within, there is room for the anchorage of five hundred ships.

This harbor is made by a great company of islands,[2] whose high cliffs shoulder out the boistrous seas, yet may easily deceive any skillful pilot, presenting many fair openings and broad sounds which afford too shallow waters for ships, though navigable for boats and small pinnaces. The entrance into the great haven is called Nantasket,[3] which is two

1. Captain John Smith (c. 1580–1631) explored the New England coast in 1614; his subsequent *Description of New England,* which included a detailed map of the area, was used by the early settlers at Plymouth and Massachusetts Bay. For the *Description* and Smith's other writings see Edward Arber and A. G. Bradley, eds., *Travels and Works of Captain John Smith* (2 vols., Edinburgh, 1910).
2. Most of the forty-odd islands in Massachusetts Bay have since washed away, been removed as navigational hazards, or used for landfill in the expansion of Boston.
3. Renamed Hull.

leagues from Boston. This place of itself is a very good haven, where ships commonly cast anchor until wind and tide serve them for other places. From hence they may sail to the river of Wessaguscus, Naponset, Charles River, and Mystic River, on which rivers be seated many towns. In any of these forenamed harbors, the seamen having spent their old store of wood and water may have fresh supplies from the adjacent islands, with good timber to repair their weather-beaten ships. Here likewise may be had masts or yards, being store of such trees as are useful for the same purpose.

CHAP. 2

Of the Seasons of the Year, Winter and Summer,
Together with the Heat, Cold, Snow, Rain,
and the Effects of It.

For that part of the country wherein most of the English have their habitations: it is for certain the best ground and sweetest climate in all those parts bearing the name of New England, agreeing well with the temper of our English bodies, being high land and sharp air. And though most of our English towns border upon the seacoast, yet are they not often troubled with mists, or unwholesome fog, or cold weather from the sea which lies east and south from the land. And whereas in England most of the cold winds and weathers come from the sea and those situations are counted most unwholesome that are near the seacoast, in that country it is not so but otherwise; for in the extremity of winter the northeast and south wind coming from the sea produceth warm weather, and bringing in the warm-working waters of the sea, looseneth the frozen bays, carrying away their ice with their tides, melting the snow, and thawing the ground. Only the northwest wind coming over the land is the cause of extreme cold weather, being always accompanied with deep snows and bitter frost, so that in two or three days the rivers are passable for horse and man. But as it is an axiom in nature, *nullum violentum est perpetuum* (no extremes last long), so this cold wind blows seldom above three days together, after which the weather is more tolerable, the air being nothing so sharp; but peradventure in four or five days after this cold messenger will blow afresh, commanding every man to his house, forbidding any to outface him without prejudice to their noses.

But it may be objected that it is too cold a country for our English men, who have been accustomed to a warmer climate. To which it may be answered (*igne levatur hyems*),[4] there is wood good store and better cheap to build warm houses and make good fires, which makes the winter less tedious. And moreover, the extremity of this cold weather lasteth but for two months or ten weeks, beginning in December and breaking up the tenth day of February, which hath been a passage very remarkable that for ten or a dozen years the weather hath held himself to his day, unlocking his icy bays and rivers which are never frozen again the same year, except there be some small frost until the middle of March.

It is observed by the Indians that every tenth year there is little or no winter, which hath been twice observed of the English: the year of New Plymouth men's arrival was no winter in comparison, and in the tenth year after, likewise, when the great company settled themselves in Massachusetts Bay was a very mild season—little frost and less snow—but clear serene weather [with] few northwest winds, which was a great mercy to the English coming over so rawly and uncomfortably provided, wanting all utensils and provisions which belonged to the well-being of planters. And whereas many died at the beginning of the plantations, it was not because the country was unhealthful but because their bodies were corrupted with sea-diet, which was naught—the beef and pork being tainted, their butter and cheese corrupted, their fish rotten—and voyage long by reason of crosswinds, so that winter approaching before they could get warm houses, and the searching sharpness of that purer climate creeping in at the crannies of their crazed bodies, caused death and sickness. But their harms having taught future voyagers more wisdom in shipping good provision for sea and finding warm houses at landing, [they] find health in both. It hath been observed that of five or six hundred passengers in one year not above three have died at sea, having their health likewise at land.

But to return to the matter in hand: daily observations makes it apparent that the piercing cold of that country produceth not so many noisome effects as the raw winters of England. In public assemblies it is

4. Wood's Latin is muddled here; he probably meant, "Winter is relieved by fire."

strange to hear a man sneeze or cough as ordinarily they do in old England. Yet not to smother anything, lest you judge me too partial in reciting good of the country and not bad, true it is that some venturing too nakedly in extremity of cold, being more foolhardy than wise, have for a time lost the use of their feet, others the use of their fingers; but time and surgery afterwards recovered them. Some have had their overgrown beards so frozen together that they could not get their strong-water bottles into their mouths. I never heard of any that utterly perished at land with cold, saving one Englishman and an Indian who going together afowling, the morning being fair at their setting out, afterward a terrible storm arising they intended to return home, but the storm being in their faces, and they not able to withstand it, were frozen to death. The Indian, having gained three flight-shot[5] more of his journey homeward, was found reared up against a tree with his aquavitae bottle at his head.

A second passage (concerning which many think hardly of the country in regard of the cold) was the miscarriage of a boat at sea. Certain men having intended a voyage to New Plymouth, setting sail towards night they wanted time to fetch it; being constrained to put into another harbor, where, being negligent of the well-mooring of their boat, a strong wind coming from the shore in the night loosened their killick and drove them to sea, without sight of land, before they had awaked out of sleep. But seeing the eminent danger, such as were not benumbed with cold shipt out their oars, shaping their course for Cape Cod where the Indians met them, who buried the dead and carried the boat with the living to Plymouth where some of them died and some recovered. These things may fright some, but being that there hath been many passages of the like nature in our English climate, it cannot dishearten such as seriously consider it, seeing likewise that their own ruins sprung from their own negligence.

The country is not so extremely cold unless it be when the northwest wind is high; at other times it is ordinary for fishermen to go to sea in January and February, in which time they get more fish, and better, than in summer, only observing to reach some good harbors before night, where by good fires they sleep as well and quietly (having their main sail tented at their backs to shelter them from the wind) as if they were at home.

5. The distance an arrow flies—approximately 200–300 yards.

To relate how some English bodies have borne out cold will (it may be) startle belief of some, it being so strange, yet not so strange as true. A certain man, being something distracted, broke away from his keeper and running into the wood could not be found with much seeking-after; but four days being expired he returned, to appearance as well in body as at his egress, and in mind much better. For a mad man to hit home through the unbeaten woods was strange, but to live without meat or drink in the deep of winter stranger, and yet return home bettered was most strange. But if truth may gain belief, you may behold a more su-perlative strangeness. A certain maid in the extremity of cold weather (as it fell out) took an uncertain journey, in her intent short—not above four miles—yet long in event; for losing her way, she wandered six or seven days in most bitter weather, not having one bit of bread to strengthen her. Sometimes a fresh spring quenched her thirst, which was all the refreshment she had. The snow being upon the ground at first, she might have tracked her own footsteps back again, but wanting that understanding, she wandered till God by his special providence brought her to the place she went from, where she lives to this day.

The hard winters are commonly the forerunners of pleasant spring-times and fertile summers, being judged likewise to make much for the health of our English bodies. It is found to be more healthful for such as shall adventure thither to come towards winter than the hot summer. The climate in winter is commonly cold and dry; the snow lies long, which is thought to be no small nourishing to the ground. For the Indi-ans burning it to suppress the underwood, which else would grow all over the country, the snow falling not long after keeps the ground warm, and with his melting conveys the ashes into the pores of the earth, which doth fatten it. It hath been observed that English wheat and rye proves better which is winter sown and is kept warm by the snow than that which is sown in the spring.

The summers be hotter than in England, because of their more south-ern latitude, yet are they tolerable, being often cooled with fresh blow-ing winds, it seldom being so hot as men are driven from their labors, especially such whose employments are within doors or under the cool shade. Servants have hitherto been privileged to rest from their labors in extreme hot weather from ten of the clock till two, which they re-gain by their early rising in the morning and double diligence in cool weather. The summers are commonly hot and dry, there being seldom any rains; I have known it six or seven weeks before one shower hath moistened the plowman's labor, yet the harvest hath been very good, the Indian corn requiring more heat than wet. For the English corn,[6] it is refreshed with the nightly dews till it grow up to shade his roots with his own substance from the parching sun.

In former times the rain came seldom but very violently, continuing his drops (which were great and many) sometimes four and twenty hours together, sometimes eight and forty, which watered the ground for a long time after. But of late the seasons be much altered, the rain coming oftener but more moderately, with lesser thunder and lightnings and sudden gusts of wind. I dare be bold to affirm it that I saw not so much rain, raw colds, and misty fogs in four years in those parts as was in England in the space of four months the last winter; yet no man at the year's end complained of too much drought or too little rain. The times of most rain are in the beginning of April and at Michaelmas.[7]

The early springs and long summers make but short autumns and winters. In the spring, when the grass begins to put forth it grows apace, so that where it was all black by reason of winter's burnings,[8] in a fortnight there will be grass a foot high.

CHAP. 3

Of the Climate, Length, and Shortness of Day and
Night, with the Suitableness of it to the English
Bodies for Health and Sickness

The country being nearer the equinoctial than England, the days and nights be more equally divided. In summer the days be two hours shorter and likewise in winter two hours longer than in England. In a word, both summer and winter is more commended of the English there than the summer-winters, and winter-summers of England. And who is there that could not wish that England's climate were as it hath been in quondam times: colder in winter and hotter in summer? Or who will condemn that which is as England hath been? Virginia having no winter to

6. I.e., wheat.
7. I.e., late September.
8. See note 26 below.

speak of, but extreme hot summers, hath dried up much English blood and by pestiferous diseases swept away many lusty bodies, changing their complexion not into swarthiness but into paleness, so that when as they come for trading into our parts we can know many of them by their faces. This alteration certainly comes not from any want of victuals or necessary food, for their soil is very fertile and pleasant, yielding both corn and cattle plenty, but rather from the climate which indeed is found to be hotter than is suitable to an ordinary English constitution.

In New England both men and women keep their natural complexions, in so much as seamen wonder when they arrive in those parts to see their countrymen so fresh and ruddy. If the sun doth tan any, yet the winter's cold restores them to their former complexion; and as it is for the outward complexion, so it is for the inward constitution, not very many being troubled with inflammations or such diseases as are increased by too much heat. And whereas I say not very many, yet dare I not exclude any: for death being certain to all, in all nations there must be something tending to death of like certainty. The soundest bodies are mortal and subject to change, therefore fall into diseases and from diseases to death.

Now the two chief messengers of mortality be fevers and calentures; but they be easily helped if taken in time and as easily prevented of any that will not prove a mere fool to his body. For the common diseases of England, they be strangers to the English now in that strange land. To my knowledge I never knew any that had the pox, measles, green-sickness, headaches, stone, or consumptions, etc. Many that have come infirm out of England retain their old grievances still, and some that were long troubled with lingering diseases, as coughs of the lungs, consumptions, etc., have been restored by that medicinable climate to their former strength and health. God hath been pleased so to bless men in the health of their bodies that I dare confidently say it: out of that town from whence I came, in three years and a half there died but three, one of which was crazed before he came into the land, the other were two children born at one birth before their time, the mother being accidentally hurt. To make good which losses I have seen four children baptized at a time, which wipes away that common aspersion that women have no children, being a mere falsity, there being as sweet, lusty children as in any other nation, and reckoning so many for so many, more double births than in England, the women likewise having a more speedy recovery and gathering of strength after their delivery than in England.

The last argument to confirm the healthfulness of the country shall be from mine own experience, who although in England I was brought up tenderly under the careful hatching of my dearest friends, yet scarce could I be acquainted with health, having been let blood six times for the pleurisy before I went, likewise being assailed with other weakening diseases; but being planted in that new soil and healthful air, which was more correspondent to my nature (I speak it with praise to the merciful God), though my occasions have been to pass through heat and cold, wet and dry, by sea and land, in winter and summer, day by day, for four days[9] together, yet scarce did I know what belonged to a day's sickness.

CHAP. 4

Of the Nature of the Soil.

The soil is for the general a warm kind of earth, there being little cold-spewing land, no moorish fens, no quagmires. The lowest grounds be the marshes, over which every full and change[10] the sea flows. These marshes be rich ground and bring plenty of hay, of which the cattle feed and like as if they were fed with the best upland hay in New England, of which likewise there is great store which grows commonly between the marshes and the woods. This meadow ground lies higher than the marshes, whereby it is freed from the overflowing of the seas; and besides this, in many places where the trees grow thin there is good fodder to be got amongst the woods. There be likewise in diverse places near the plantations great broad meadows, wherein grow neither shrub nor tree, lying low, in which plains grows as much grass as may be thrown out with a scythe, thick and long, as high as a man's middle, some as high as the shoulders, so that a good mower may cut three loads

9. Although the 1635 and 1639 editions read "days," Wood must have intended "years," the period he was in New England. The 1634 edition has "years."
10. Wood's meaning is not clear. He probably referred to changes in the tide at full moon and new moon.

in a day. But many object, this is but a coarse fodder. True it is that it is not so fine to the eye as English grass, but it is not sour, though it grow thus rank, but being made into hay the cattle eat it as well as it were lea hay[11] and like as well with it. I dare not think England can show fairer cattle either in winter or summer than is in those parts both winter and summer, being generally larger and better of milch, and bring forth young as ordinarily as cattle do in England and have hitherto been free from many diseases that are incident to cattle in England.

To return to the subject in hand, there is so much hay ground in the country as the richest voyagers that shall venture thither need not fear want of fodder, though his herd increase into thousands, there being thousands of acres that yet was never meddled with. And whereas it hath been reported that some hath mown a day for half of a load of hay, I do not say, but it may be true. A man may do as much and get as little in England on Salisbury Plain or in other places where grass cannot be expected. So hay ground is not in all places in New England. Wherefore it shall behoove every man according to his calling and estate to look for a fit situation at the first, and if he be one that intends to live on his stock, to choose the grassy valleys before the woody mountains. Furthermore, whereas it hath been generally reported in many places of England that the grass grows not in those places where it was cut the foregoing years, it is a mere falsehood, for it grows as well the ensuing spring as it did before and is more speary[12] and thick, like our English grass. And in such places where the cattle use to graze, the ground is much improved in the woods, growing more grassy and less weedy. The worst that can be said against the meadow grounds is because there is little eddish[13] or after-pasture, which may proceed from the late mowing more than from anything else; but though the eddish be not worth much, yet is there such plenty of other grass and feeding that there is no want of winter fodder till December, at which time men begin to house their milch cattle and calves. Some, notwithstanding the cold of the winter, have their young cattle without doors, giving them meat[14] at morning and at evening. For the more upland grounds, there be different kinds: in some places clay, some gravel, some

11. I.e., hay from a meadowland, or cultivated hay.
12. Hard, stiff.
13. Grass that grows in a field after mowing.
14. Wood here uses "meat" in the sense of food or nourishment.

red sand, all which are covered with a black mold, in some places above a foot deep, in other places not so deep. There be very few that have the experience of the ground that can condemn it of barrenness, although many deem it barren because the English use to manure their land with fish, which they do not because the land could not bring corn without it but because it brings more with it; the land likewise being kept in heart[15] the longer. Besides, the plenty of fish which they have for little or nothing is better so used than cast away. But to argue the goodness of the ground, the Indians who are too lazy to catch fish plant corn eight or ten years in one place without it, having very good crops.[16] Such is the rankness of the ground that it must be sown the first year with Indian corn, which is a soaking grain, before it will be fit for to receive English seed. In a word, as there is no ground so purely good as the long forced and improved grounds of England, so is there none so extremely bad as in many places of England that as yet have not been manured and improved, the woods of New England being accounted better ground than the forests of England, or woodland ground, or heathy plains.

For the natural soil, I prefer it before the country of Surrey or Middlesex, which if they were not enriched with continual manurings would be less fertile than the meanest ground in New England. Wherefore it is neither impossible, nor much improbable, that upon improvements the soil may be as good in time as England. And whereas some gather the ground to be naught, and soon out of heart because Plymouth men remove from their old habitations, I answer: they do no more remove from their habitation than the citizen which hath one house in the city and another in the country for his pleasure, health, and profit. For although they have taken new plots of ground and build houses upon them, yet do they retain their old houses still, and repair to them every Sabbath day; neither do they esteem their old lots worse than when they first took them. What if they do not plant on them every year? I hope it is no ill husbandry to rest the land, nor is always that the worst that lies sometimes fallow. If any man doubt of the goodness of the ground, let him comfort himself with the cheapness of it. Such bad land in England,

15. I.e., fertile.
16. The long-held assumption that the Indians fertilized their crops with fish has recently been challenged. See Lynn Ceci, "Fish Fertilizer: A Native North American Practice?" *Science*, 188 (April 1975), 26–30, which argues that the use of fish fertilizer was native to Europe, not America.

I am sure, will bring in store of good money. This ground is in some places of a soft mold and easy to plow; in other places so tough and hard that I have seen ten oxen toiled, their iron chains broken, and their shares and colters much strained. But after the first breaking up it is so easy that two oxen and a horse may plow it. There hath as good English corn grown there as could be desired, especially rye and oats and barley. There hath been no great trial as yet of wheat and beans. Only thus much I affirm: that these two grains grow well in gardens, therefore it is not improbable but when they can gather seed of that which is sown in the country, it may grow as well as any other grain. But commonly the seed that cometh out of England is heated at sea and therefore cannot thrive at land.[17]

CHAP. 5

Of the Herbs, Fruits, Woods, Waters, and Minerals.

The ground affords very good kitchen gardens for turnips, parsnips, carrots, radishes, and pumpions,[18] muskmellon, isquouterquashes,[19] cucumbers, onions, and whatsoever grows well in England grows as well there, many things being better and larger. There is likewise growing all manner of herbs for meat and medicine, and that not only in planted gardens but in the woods, without either the art or the help of man, as sweet marjoram, purslane, sorrell, penerial,[20] yarrow, myrtle, sarsaparilla,[21] bays, etc. There is likewise strawberries in abundance, very large ones, some being two inches about; one may gather half a bushel in a forenoon. In other seasons there be gooseberries, bilberries, raspberries,

17. On agricultural practices in England and New England see Joan Thirsk, *Agrarian History of England and Wales,* 4 (London, 1967); Darrett B. Rutman *Husbandmen of Plymouth* (Boston, 1967); and Percy W. Bidwell and John I. Falconer, *History of Agriculture in the Northern United States, 1620–1860* (Washington, 1925). A useful recent geographical study is Douglass McManis, *Colonial New England: A Historical Geography* (New York, 1975).
18. A variant spelling of pumpkins.
19. Sometimes spelled *askoot-asquash,* the Algonquian word for squashes, of which there were several varieties.
20. An obsolete form of "pennyroyal."
21. Wood here spelled it "saxifarilla." Early explorers and colonists used several versions of the word.

treackleberries,[22] hurtleberries, currants—which being dried in the sun are little inferior to those that our grocers sell in England. This land likewise affords hemp and flax, some naturally and some planted by the English, with rapes if they be well managed.

For such commodities as lie underground, I cannot out of mine own experience or knowledge say much, having taken no great notice of such things, but it is certainly reported that there is ironstone; and the Indians inform us that they can lead us to the mountains of black lead and have shown us lead ore, if our small judgment in such things do not deceive us. And though nobody dare confidently conclude, yet dare they not utterly deny, but that the Spaniards' bliss[23] may lie hid in the barren mountains. Such as have coasted the country affirm that they know where to fetch seacoal if wood were scant. There is plenty of stone, both rough and smooth, useful for many things, with quarries of slate out of which they get covering for houses, with good clay whereof they make tiles and bricks and pavements for their necessary uses.

For the country, it is as well watered as any land under the sun, every family or every two families having a spring of sweet waters betwixt them, which is far different from the waters of England, being not so sharp but of a fatter substance and of a more jetty color. It is thought there can be no better water in the world. Yet dare I not prefer it before good beer as some have done, but any man will choose it before bad beer, whey, or buttermilk. Those that drink it be as healthful, fresh, and lusty as they that drink beer.[24] These springs be not only within land but likewise bordering upon the seacoasts, so that sometimes the tides overflow some of them, which is accounted rare in the most parts of England. No man hitherto hath been constrained to dig deep for his water, or to fetch it far, or to fetch of several waters for several uses, one kind of water serving for washing and brewing and other things. Now besides these springs there be diverse spacious ponds in many places of

22. Mentioned also by John Josselyn *New-England's Rarities Discovered* (London, 1672; repr. American Antiquarian Society, *Transactions and Collections,* 4 [1860], 176. A berry of supposed medicinal value.

23. I.e., gold.

24. Beer was a widely used beverage for Englishmen of all ages and classes; its absence in early New England perturbed some prospective settlers who feared that water was not safe to drink, as was often the case at home. See Dean Albertson, "Puritan Liquor in the Planting of New England," *New England Quarterly,* 23 (1950), 477-490.

the country, out of which run many sweet streams which are constant in their course both winter and summer, whereat the cattle quench their thirst and upon which may be built water mills as the plantation increases.

The next commodity the land affords is good store of woods, and that not only such as may be needful for fuel but likewise for the building of ships and houses and mills and all manner of water-work about which wood is needful. The timber of the country grows straight and tall, some trees being twenty, some thirty foot high, before they spread forth their branches; generally the trees be not very thick, though there may be many that will serve for mill posts, some being three foot and a half over. And whereas it is generally conceived that the woods grow so thick that there is no more clear ground than is hewed out by labor of man, it is nothing so, in many places diverse acres being clear so that one may ride ahunting in most places of the land if he will venture himself for being lost. There is no underwood saving in swamps and low grounds that are wet, in which the English get osiers and hasles[25] and such small wood as is for their use. Of these swamps, some be ten, some twenty, some thirty miles long, being preserved by the wetness of the soil wherein they grow; for it being the custom of the Indians to burn the wood in November when the grass is withered and leaves dried, it consumes all the underwood and rubbish which otherwise would overgrow the country, making it unpassable, and spoil their much affected hunting; so that by this means in those places where the Indians inhabit there is scarce a bush or bramble or any cumbersome underwood to be seen in the more champion ground.[26] Small wood, growing in these places where the fire could not come, is preserved. In some places, where the Indians died of the plague some fourteen years ago, is much underwood, as in the midway betwixt Wessaguscus and Plymouth, because it hath not been burned. Certain rivers stopping the fire from coming to clear that place of the country hath made it unuseful and troublesome

25. Obsolete form of hazel.
26. Indians in the northeast commonly burned the underbrush in heavily forested areas. Among the reasons for this practice were driving wild game into the open and easing travel. See Gordon M. Day, "The Indians as an Ecological Factor in the Northeast Forest," *Ecology*, 32 (1954), 329–346; and Calvin Martin, "Fire and Forest Structure in the Aboriginal Eastern Forest," *The Indian Historian*, 6 (1973), 23–26. See also pp. 30–31 above.

to travel through, insomuch that it is called ragged plain because it tears and rents the clothes of them that pass.

Now because it may be necessary for mechanical artificers to know what timber and wood of use is in the country, I will recite the most useful as followeth:

> Trees both in hills and plains in plenty be,
> The long-lived oak and mournful cypress tree,
> Sky-towering pines, and chestnuts coated rough,
> The lasting cedar, with the walnut tough;
> The rosin-dropping fir for masts in use,
> The boatmen seek for oars light, neat-grown spruce,
> The brittle ash, the ever-trembling asps,
> The broad-spread elm whose concave harbors wasps,
> The water-spungy alder good for nought,
> Small eldern by the Indian fletchers sought,
> The knotty maple, pallid birch, hawthorns;
> The horn-bound tree that to be cloven scorns,
> Which from the tender vine oft take his spouse,
> Who twinds embracing arms about his boughs.
> Within this Indian orchard fruits be some,
> The ruddy cherry and the jetty plumb,
> Snake-murthering hazel, with sweet saxifrage,
> Whose spurns in beer allays hot fever's rage.
> The dyer's sumac,[27] with more trees there be,
> That are both good to use, and rare to see.

Though many of these trees may seem to have epithets contrary to the nature of them as they grow in England, yet are they agreeable with the trees of that country. The chief and common timber for ordinary use is oak and walnut. Of oaks there be three kinds: the red oak, white and black. As these are different in kind, so are they chosen for such uses as they are most fit for, one kind being more fit for clapboard, others for sawn board, some fitter for shipping, others for houses. These trees afford much mast for hogs, especially every third year, bearing a bigger acorn than our English oak. The walnut tree is something different from

27. Wood's spelling was "diars shumach"; he probably meant the species used to dye leather, hence "dyer's sumac."

the English walnut, being a great deal more tough and more serviceable and altogether as heavy; and whereas our guns that are stocked with English walnut are soon broken and cracked in frost, being a brittle wood, we are driven to stock them new with the country walnut, which will endure all blows and weather, lasting time out of mind. These trees bear a very good nut, something smaller but nothing inferior in sweetness and goodness to the English nut, having no bitter pill. There is likewise a tree in some part of the country that bears a nut as big as a small pear.

The cedar tree is a tree of no great growth, not bearing above a foot and a half square at the most, neither is it very high. I suppose they be much inferior to the cedars of Lebanon so much commended in holy writ. This wood is more desired for ornament than substance, being of color red and white like eugh,[28] smelling as sweet as juniper; it is commonly used for sealing of houses and making of chests, boxes, and staves,

The fir and pine be trees that grow in many places, shooting up exceeding high, especially the pine. They do afford good masts, good board, rosin and turpentine. Out of these pines is gotten the candlewood that is so much spoken of, which may serve for a shift amongst poor folks; but I cannot commend it for singular good because it is something sluttish, dropping a pitchy kind of substance where it stands. Here no doubt might be good done with sawmills, for I have seen of these stately high-grown trees ten miles together close by the river side, from whence by shipping they might be conveyed to any desired port. Likewise it is not improbable that pitch and tar may be forced from these trees which bear no other kind of fruit.

For that country ash, it is much different from the ash of England, being brittle and good for little, so that walnut is used for it. The hornbound tree[29] is a tough kind of wood that requires so much pains in riving as is almost incredible, being the best for to make bowls and dishes, not being subject to crack or leak. This tree growing with broad spread arms, the vines wind their curling branches about them, which vines afford great store of grapes which are very big both for the grape and cluster, sweet and good.

28. Obsolete form of "yew."
29. Probably refers to the blue beach, sometimes called horn-beech, horn beam, or hard beam.

These [grapes] be of two sorts, red and white; there is likewise a smaller kind of grape which groweth in the islands which is sooner ripe and more delectable, so that there is no known reason why as good wine may not be made in those parts as well as in Bordeaux in France, being under the same degree. It is great pity no man sets upon such a venture, whereby he might in small time enrich himself and benefit the country. I know nothing which doth hinder but want of skillfull men to manage such an employment. For the country is hot enough, the ground good enough, and many convenient hills which lie toward the south sun as if they were there placed for the purpose.

The cherry trees yield great store of cherries, which grow on clusters like grapes; they be much smaller than our English cherry, nothing near so good if they be not very ripe. They so fur the mouth that the tongue will cleave to the roof and the throat wax hoarse with swallowing those red bullies (as I may call them), being little better in taste. English ordering may bring them to be an English cherry, but yet they are as wild as the Indians.

The plums of the country be better for plums than the cherries be for cherries; they be black and yellow about the bigness of a damson, of a reasonable good taste. The white thorn affords haws as big as an English cherry, which is esteemed above a cherry for his goodness and pleasantness to the taste.

CHAP. 6

Of the Beasts that Live on the Land.

Having related unto you the pleasant situation of the country, the healthfulness of the climate, the nature of the soil, with his vegetatives and other commodities, it will not be amiss to inform you of such irrational creatures as are daily bred and continually nourished in this country, which do much conduce to the well-being of the inhabitants, affording not only meat for the belly but clothing for the back. The beasts be as followeth:

> The kingly lion and the strong-armed bear,
> The large-limbed mooses, with the tripping deer,

Quill-darting porcupines, and racoons be
Castled in the hollow of an aged tree;
The skipping squirrel, rabbit, purblind hare,
Immured in the selfsame castle are,
Lest red-eyed ferrets, wily foxes should
Them undermine, if rampired but with mold.
The grim-faced ounce, and ravenous, howling wolf,
Whose meagre paunch sucks like a swallowing gulf.
Black, glistering otters and rich-coated beaver,
The civet-scented musquash smelling ever.

Concerning lions, I will not say that I ever saw any myself, but some affirm that they have seen a lion at Cape Ann, which is not above six leagues from Boston. Some likewise being lost in woods have heard such terrible roarings as have made them much aghast, which must either be devils or lions, there being no other creatures which use to roar saving bears, which have not such a terrible kind of roaring. Besides, Plymouth men have traded for lions' skins in former times. But sure it is that there be lions on that continent, for the Virginians saw an old lion in their plantation, who having lost his jackal, which was wont to hunt his prey, was brought so poor that he could go no further.[30]

For bears, they be common, being a great black kind of bear which be most fierce in strawberry time, at which time they have young ones. At this time likewise they will go upright like a man, and climb trees, and swim to the islands; which if the Indians see, there will be more sportful bear-baiting than Paris Garden can afford. For seeing the bears take water, an Indian will leap after him, where they go to water cuffs for bloody noses and scratched sides; in the end the man gets the victory, riding the bear over the watery plain till he can bear him no longer. In the winter they take themselves to the clefts of rocks and thick swamps to shelter them from the cold; and food being scant in those cold and hard times, they live only by sleeping and sucking their paws, which keepeth them as fat as they are in summer. There would be more of them if it were not for the wolves, which devour them. A kennel of those ravening runnagadoes[31] setting on a poor single bear will tear him as a dog will tear a kid.

30. There were no lions in New England, but rumors of them long persisted.
31. I.e., renegades.

It would be a good change if the country had for every wolf a bear, upon the condition all the wolves were banished; so should the inhabitants be not only rid of their greatest annoyance but furnished with more store of provisions, bears being accounted very good meat, esteemed of all men above venison. Again they never prey upon the English cattle, or offer to assault the person of any man, unless being vexed with a shot, and a man run upon them before they be dead, in which case they will stand in their own defence, as may appear by this instance. Two men going afowling, appointed at evening to meet at a certain pond side to share equally and to return home; one of these gunners having killed a seal or sea calf brought it to the pond where he was to meet his comrade, afterwards returning to the seaside for more gain; and having loaded himself with more geese and ducks, he repaired to the pond where he saw a great bear feeding on his seal, which caused him to throw down his load and give the bear a salute; which, though it was but with goose shot, yet tumbled him over and over, whereupon the man, supposing him to be in a manner dead, ran and beat him with the hand of his gun. The bear perceiving him to be such a coward to strike him when he was down, scrambled up, standing at defiance with him, scratching his legs, tearing his clothes and face, who stood it out till his six foot gun was broken in the middle. Then being deprived of his weapon, he ran up to the shoulders into the pond where he remained till the bear was gone and his mate come in, who accompanied him home.

The beast called a moose is not much unlike red deer. This beast is as big as an ox, slow of foot, headed like a buck, with a broad beam, some being two yards wide in the head. Their flesh is as good as beef, their hides good for clothing. The English have some thoughts of keeping them tame and to accustom them to the yoke, which will be a great commodity: first, because they are so fruitful, bringing forth three at a time, being likewise very uberous;[32] secondly, because they will live in winter without fodder. There be not many of these in the Massachusetts Bay, but forty miles to the northeast there be great store of them. These poor beasts likewise are much devoured by the wolves.

The ordinary deer be much bigger than the deer of England, of a brighter color, more inclining to red, with spotted bellies. The most store of these be in winter, when the more northern parts of the country

32. Supplying milk or nourishment in abundance.

be cold for them. They desire to be near the sea, so that they may swim to the island when they are chased by the wolves. It is not to be thought into what great multitudes they would increase were it not for the common devourer, the wolf. They have generally three [calves] at a time, which they hide a mile one from another, giving them suck by turns. Thus they do, that if the wolf should find one he might miss of the other. These deer be fat in the deep of winter. In summer it is hard catching of them with the best greyhounds that may be procured because they be swift of foot. Some credible persons have affirmed that they have seen a deer leap threescore feet at little or no forcement; besides, there be so many old trees, rotten stumps, and Indian barns, that a dog cannot well run without being shoulder-shot. Yet would I not dissuade any from carrying good dogs, for in the wintertime they be very useful, for when the snow is hard frozen, the deer being heavy sinks into the snow; the dogs being light run upon the top and overtake them and pull them down. Some by this means have gotten twenty bucks and does in a winter. The horns of these deer grow in a straight manner (overhanging their heads) that they cannot feed upon such things as grow low till they have cast their old horns. Of these deer there be a great many, and more in the Massachusetts Bay than in any other place, which is a great help and refreshment to those planters.

The porcupine is a small thing not much unlike a hedgehog, something bigger, who stands upon his guard and proclaims a *noli me tangere*[33] to man and beast that shall approach too near him, darting his quills into their legs and hides. The raccoon is a deep-furred beast, not much unlike a badger, having a tail like a fox, as good meat as a lamb; there is one of them in the Tower.[34] These beasts in the daytime sleep in hollow trees, in the moonshine night they go to feed on clams at a low tide by the seaside, where the English hunt them with their dogs.

The squirrels be of three sorts: first the great gray squirrel, which is almost as big as an English rabbit. Of these there be the greatest plenty; one may kill a dozen of them in an afternoon—about three of the clock they begin to walk. The second is a small squirrel, not unlike the English squirrel, which doth much trouble the planters of corn, so that they are constrained to set diverse traps and to carry their cats into the corn fields till their corn be three weeks old. The third kind is a flying squir-

33. Transl.: "Do not touch me."
34. The Tower of London, where specimens of exotic American fauna were kept.

rel which is not very big, slender of body, with a great deal of loose skin which she spreads when she flies, which the wind gets and so wafts her batlike body from place to place. It is a creature more for sight and wonderment than either pleasure and profit.

The rabbits be much like ours in England. The hares be some of them white and a yard long; these two harmless creatures are glad to shelter themselves from the harmful foxes in hollow trees having a hole at the entrance no bigger than they can creep in at. If they should make them holes in the ground, as our English rabbits do, the undermining re-noilds[35] would rob them of their lives and extirpate their generation.

The beasts of offence be skunks, ferrets, foxes, whose impudence sometimes drives them to the goodwives' hen roost to fill their paunch. Some of these be black; their fur is of much esteem.

The ounce or the wildcat[36] is as big as a mongrel dog. This creature is by nature fierce and more dangerous to be met withal than any other creature, not fearing either dog or man. He useth to kill deer, which he thus effecteth: knowing the deer's tracts, he will lie lurking in long weeds, the deer passing by he suddenly leaps upon his back, from thence gets to his neck and scratcheth out his throat. He hath likewise a device to get geese, for being much of the color of a goose he will place himself close by the water, holding up his bob tail, which is like a goose neck; the geese seeing this counterfeiting goose approach nigh to visit him, who with a sudden jerk apprehends his mistrustless prey. The English kill many of those, accounting them very good meat. Their skins be a very deep kind of fur, spotted white and black on the belly.

The wolves be in some respect different from them in other countries. It was never known yet that a wolf ever set upon a man or woman. Neither do they trouble horses or cows; but swine, goats, and red calves, which they take for deer, be often destroyed by them, so that a red calf is cheaper than a black one in that regard in some places. In the time of autumn and in the beginning of spring, these ravenous rangers do most frequent our English habitations, following the deer which come down at that time to those parts. They be made much like a mongrel, being big boned, lank paunched, deep breasted, having a thick neck and head,

35. I.e., reynards, foxes.
36. Marginal note in 1635 ed.: "This beast is called a luzeran, of the same kind of fur that our rich Parliament robes are lined, but not so good a fur as in other, more northern, parts."

prick ears, and long snout, with dangerous teeth, long-staring hair, and a great bush tail. It is thought of many that our English mastiffs might be too hard for them; but it is no such matter, for they care no more for an ordinary mastiff than an ordinary mastiff cares for a cur. Many good dogs have been spoiled by them. Once a fair greyhound, hearing them at their howlings, run out to chide them, who was torn in pieces before he could be rescued. One of them makes no more bones to run away with a pig than a dog to run away with a marrow bone. It is observed that they have no joints from their head to the tail, which prevents them from leaping, or sudden turning, as may appear by what I shall show you.

A certain man having shot a wolf as he was feeding upon a swine, breaking his leg only, he knew not how to devise his death on a sudden. The wolf being a black one, he was loath to spoil his fur with a second shot, his skin being worth five or six pound sterling. Wherefore he resolved to get him by the tail and thrust him into a river that was hard by; which effected, the wolf being not able to turn his jointless body to bite him, was taken. That they cannot leap may appear by this wolf, whose mouth watering at a few poor impaled kids, would needs leap over a five-footed pale to be at them; but his foot slipping in the rise, he fell short of his desire, and being hung in the carpenters' stocks howled so loud that he frighted away the kids and called the English, who killed him.

These be killed daily in some place or other, either by the English or Indian, who have a certain rate for every head. Yet is there little hope of their utter destruction, the country being so spacious and they so numerous, travelling in the swamps by kennels. Sometimes ten or twelve are of a company. Late at night and early in the morning they set up their howlings and call their companies together—at night to hunt, at morning to sleep. In a word they be the greatest inconveniency the country hath, both for matter of damage to private men in particular, and the whole country in general.

CHAP. 7

Beasts Living in the Water.

For all creatures that lived both by land and water, they be first otters, which be most of them black, whose fur is much used for muffs and are held almost as dear as beaver. The flesh of them is none of the best meat, but their oil is of rare use for many things. Secondly, martins, a good fur for their bigness. Thirdly, musquashes, which be much like a beaver for shape, but nothing near so big. The male hath two stones which smell as sweet as musk, and being killed in winter and the spring, never lose their sweet smell. These skins are no bigger than a cony skin,[37] yet are sold for five shillings apiece, being sent for tokens into England. One good skin will perfume a whole house full of clothes if it be right and good. Fourthly, the beaver, concerning whom, if I should at large discourse according to knowledge or information, I might make a volume.

The wisdom and understanding of this beast will almost conclude him a reasonable creature. His shape is thick and short, having likewise short legs, feet like a mole before and behind like a goose, a broad tail in form like a shoe sole, very tough and strong. His head is something like an otter's head, saving that his teeth before be placed like the teeth of a rabbit, two above and two beneath, sharp and broad, with which he cuts down trees as thick as a man's thigh, sometimes as big as a man's body, afterwards dividing them into lengths according to the use they are appointed for. If one beaver be too weak to carry the log, then another helps him; if they two be too weak, then *multorum manibus grande levatur onus,*[38] four more adding their help, being placed three to three, which set their teeth in one another's tough tails, and laying the load on the two hindmost, they draw the log to the desired place, also tow it in the water, the strongest getting under, bearing it up that it may swim the lighter. That this may not seem altogether incredible, remember that the like almost may be seen in our ants, which will join sometimes seven or eight together in the carrying of a burthen.

37. In the seventeenth century "cony" referred to adult rabbits; "rabbits" usually pertained only to the young of the species, though usage was inconsistent.
38. Transl.: "A heavy weight is lifted by the hands of many," or more loosely, "Many hands make light work."

These creatures build themselves houses of wood and clay close by the pond's side, and knowing the seasons build them answerable houses, having them three stories high so that as land-floods are raised by great rains, as the water arise they mount higher in their houses; as they assuage they descend lower again. These houses are so strong that no creature saving an industrious man with his penetrating tools can prejudice them, their ingress and egress being under water. These make likewise very good ponds, knowing whence a stream runs from between two rising hills they will there pitch down piles of wood, placing smaller rubbish before it with clay and sods, not leaving till by their art and industry they have made a firm and curious damhead which may draw admiration from wise, understanding men.

These creatures keep themselves to their own families, never parting so long as they are able to keep house together. And it is commonly said, if any beaver accidentally light into a strange place, he is made a drudge so long as he lives there, to carry at the greater end of the log, unless he creep away by stealth. Their wisdom secures them from the English who seldom or never kills any of them, being not patient to lay a long siege or to be so often deceived by their cunning evasions, so that all the beaver which the English have comes first from the Indians whose time and experience fits them for that employment.

CHAP. 8

Of the Birds and Fowls Both of Land and Water.

Having showed you the most desirable, useful, and beneficial creatures, with the most offensive carrions that belong to our wilderness, it remains in the next place to show you such kinds of fowl as the country affords. They are many, and we have much variety both at sea and on land, and such as yield us much profit and honest pleasure, and are these that follow; as

> The princely eagle, and the soaring hawk,
> Whom in their unknown ways there's none can chalk:
> The humbird for some queen's rich cage more fit,
> Than in the vacant widerness to sit.

The swift-winged swallow sweeping to and fro,
As swift as arrow from Tartarian bow.
When as Aurora's infant day new springs,
There the morning mounting lark her sweet lays sings.
The harmonious thrush, swift pigeon, turtledove,
Who to her mate doth ever constant prove.
The turkey-pheasant, heathcock, partridge rare,
The carrion-tearing crow, and hurtful stare,
The long-lived raven, the ominous screech-owl,
Who tells, as old wives say, disasters foul.
The drowsy madge that leaves her day-loved nest,
And loves to rove when day-birds be at rest;
The eel-murthering hearn, and greedy cormorant,
That near the creeks in moorish marshes haunt.
The bellowing bittern, with the long-legged crane,
Presaging winters hard, and dearth of grain.
The silver swan that tunes her mournful breath,
To sing the dirge of her approaching death.
The tatling oldwives, and the cackling geese,
The fearful gull that shuns the murthering piece.
The strong winged mallard, with the nimble teal,
And ill-shaped loon who his harsh notes doth squeal.
There widgins, sheldrackes, and humilites,
Snites, doppers, sea-larks, in whole millions flee.[39]

The eagles of the country be of two sorts, one like the eagles that be in England, the other is something bigger with a great white head and white tail. These be commonly called gripes; they prey upon ducks and geese and such fish as are cast upon the seashore. And although an eagle be counted king of that feathered regiment, yet is there a certain black hawk that beats him so that he is constrained to soar so high till heat expel his adversary. This hawk is much prized of the Indians, being accounted a sagamore's ransom.

To speak much of hawks were to trespass upon my own judgment

39. For descriptions of the various birds mentioned by Wood, see below and two works by John Josselyn: *New-Englands Rarities Discovered,* and *An Account of Two Voyages to New-England* (London, 1675; repr. Massachusetts Historical Society, *Collections,* 3rd ser. 3 [1833]).

and bring upon myself a deserved censure for abusing the falconer's terms. But by relation from those that have more insight into them than myself, there be diverse kinds of hawks. Their aeries are easy to come by, being in the holes of rocks near the shore, so that any who are addicted to that sport—if he will be but at the charge of finding poultry for them—may have his desires. We could wish them well mewed in England, for they make havoc of hens, partridges, heathcocks, and ducks, often hindering the fowler of his long looked-for shoot.

The humbird is one of the wonders of the country, being no bigger than a hornet, yet hath all the dimensions of a bird, as bill and wings, with quills, spider-like legs, small claws. For color, she is as glorious as the rainbow. As she flies, she makes a little humming noise like a humble-bee: wherefore she is called the humbird.

The pigeon of that country is something different from our dove-house pigeons in England, being more like turtles, of the same color. They have long tails like a magpie. And they seem not so big, because they carry not so many feathers on their backs as our English doves, yet are they as big in body. These birds come into the country to go to the north parts in the beginning of our spring, at which time (if I may be counted worthy to be believed in a thing that is not so strange as true) I have seen them fly as if the airy regiment had been pigeons, seeing neither beginning nor ending, length or breadth of these millions of millions. The shouting of people, the rattling of guns, and pelting of small shot could not drive them out of their course, but so they continued for four or five hours together. Yet it must not be concluded that it is thus often, for it is but at the beginning of the spring, and at Michaelmas when they return back to the southward; yet are there some all the year long, which are easily attained by such as look after them. Many of them build amongst the pine trees, thirty miles to the northeast of our plantations, joining nest to nest and tree to tree by their nests, so that the sun never sees the ground in that place, from whence the Indians fetch whole loads of them.

The turkey is a very large bird, of a black color yet white in flesh, much bigger than our English turkey. He hath the use of his long legs so ready that he can run as fast as a dog and fly as well as a goose. Of these sometimes there will be forty, threescore, and an hundred of a flock, sometimes more and sometimes less. Their feeding is acorns, haws and berries; some of them get a haunt to frequent our English corn. In winter when the snow covers the ground, they resort to the seashore to look for shrimps and such small fishes at low tides. Such as love turkey hunting must follow it in winter after a new fallen snow, when he may follow them by their tracks. Some have killed ten or a dozen in half a day. If they can be found towards an evening and watched where they perch, if one come about ten or eleven of the clock, he may shoot as often as he will; they will sit unless they be slenderly wounded. These turkey remain all the year long. The price of a good turkey cock is four shillings, and he is well worth it, for he may be in weight forty pound, a hen two shillings.

Pheasants be very rare, but heathcocks and partridges be common. He that is a husband,[40] and will be stirring betime, may kill half a dozen in a morning. The partridges be bigger than they be in England. The flesh of the heathcocks is red and the flesh of a partridge white; their price is four pence apiece.

The ravens and the crows be much like them of other countries. There are no magpies, jackdaws, cuckoos, jays, sparrows, etc. The stares be bigger than those in England, as black as crows, being the most troublesome and injurious bird of all others, pulling up the corns by the roots when it is young so that those who plant by reedy and seggy[41] places, where they frequent, are much annoyed with them, they being so audacious that they fear not guns or their fellows hung upon poles. But the corn having a week or nine days growth is post their spoiling. The owls be of two sorts: the one being small, speckled like a partridge, with ears; the other being a great owl, almost as big as an eagle, his body being as good meat as a partridge.

Cormorants be as common as other fowls, which destroy abundance of small fish. These be not worth the shooting because they are the worst of fowls for meat, tasting rank and fishy. Again, one may shoot twenty times and miss, for seeing the fire in the pan, they dive under the water before the shot comes to the place where they were. They use[d] to roost upon the tops of trees and rocks, being a very heavy drowsy creature, so that the Indians will go in their canoes in the night and take them from the rocks as easily as women take a hen from roost. No ducking ponds can afford more delight than a lame cormorant and two or three lusty dogs.

40. I.e., a farmer; especially, in this instance, a prudent provider of his family.
41. Obsolete variation of "sedgy," i.e., covered with coarse grass and shrubs.

The crane, although he be almost as tall as a man by reason of his long legs and neck, yet is his body rounder than other fowls, not much unlike the body of a turkey. I have seen many of these fowls, yet did I never see one that was fat—though very sleeky. I suppose it is contrary to their nature to grow fat. Of these there be many in summer but none in winter. Their price is two shillings. There be likewise many swans which frequent the fresh ponds and rivers, seldom consorting themselves with ducks and geese. These be very good meat; the price of one is six shillings.

The geese of the country be of three sorts: first a brant goose, which is a goose almost like the wild goose in England; the price of one of these is six pence. The second kind is a white goose, almost as big as an English tame goose. These come in great flocks about Michaelmas. Sometimes there will be two or three thousand in a flock; those continue six weeks and so fly to the southward, returning in March and staying six weeks more, returning again to the northward. The price of one of these is eight pence. The third kind of geese is a great gray goose with a black neck and a black and white head, strong of flight, and these be a great deal bigger than the ordinary geese of England, some very fat, and in the spring so full of feathers that the shot can scarce pierce them. Most of these geese remain with us from Michaelmas to April. They feed on the sea, upon grass in the bays at low water and gravel, and in the woods of acorns, having as other fowl have their pass and repass to the northward and southward. The accurate marksmen kill of these both flying and sitting; the price of a good gray goose is eighteen pence.

The ducks of the country be very large ones and in great abundance, so is there of teal likewise. The price of a duck is six pence, of a teal three pence. If I should tell you how some have killed a hundred geese in a week, fifty ducks at a shot, forty teals at another, it may be counted impossible though nothing more certain.

The oldwives be a foul that never leave tatling day or night, something bigger than a duck. The loon is an ill-shaped thing like a cormorant, but that he can neither go nor fly. He maketh a noise sometimes like a sowgelder's horn. The humilities or simplicities (as I may rather call them) be of two sorts, the biggest being as big as a green plover, the other as big as birds that we call knots in England. Such is the simplicity of the smaller sorts of these birds that one may drive them on a heap like so many sheep, and seeing a fit time shoot them. The living seeing the dead, settle themselves on the same place again, amongst which the fowler discharges again. I myself have killed twelve score at two shoots. These bird are to be had upon sandy brakes at the latter end of summer before the geese come in.

Thus much have I showed you as I know to be true concerning the fowl of the country. But methinks I hear some say that this is very good if it could be caught, or likely to continue, and that much shooting will fright away the fowls. True it is that everyone's employment will not permit him to fowl: what then? Yet their employments furnish them with silver guns with which they may have it more easy. For the frighting of the fowl, true it is that many go blurting away their powder and shot that have no more skill to kill or win a goose than many in England that have rusty muskets in their houses knows what belongs to a soldier, yet are they not much afrighted. I have seen more living and dead the last year than I have done in former years.

CHAP. 9

Of Fish.

Having done with these, let me lead you from the land to the sea, to view what commodities may come from thence. There is no country known that yields more variety of fish winter and summer, and that not only for the present spending and sustenation of the plantations, but likewise for trade into other countries, so that those which have had stages and make fishing voyages into those parts have gained (it is thought) more than the Newfoundland fishermen. Codfish in these seas are larger than in Newfoundland, six or seven making a quintal, whereas there they have fifteen to the same weight; and though this they seem a base and more contemptible commodity in the judgement of more neat adventurers, yet it hath been the enrichment of other nations and is likely to prove no small commodity to the planters, and likewise to England if it were thoroughly undertaken. At this time being yearly used, a great return is made to the West Country merchants of Bristol, Plymouth, and Barnstable. Salt may be had from the salt islands and, as is supposed, may be made in the country. The chief fish for trade is cod, but for the use of the country there is all manner of fish as followeth.

The king of waters, the sea-shouldering whale,
The snuffing grampus, with the oily seal,
The storm-presaging porpus, herring-hog,
Line-shearing shark, the catfish, and sea dog,
The scale-fenced sturgeon, wry-mouthed halibut,
The flounsing salmon, codfish, greedigut:
Cole, haddock, hake, the thornback, and the skate,
Whose slimy outside makes him selde[42] in date,
The stately bass old Neptune's fleeting post,
That tides it out and in from sea to coast.
Consorting herrings, and the bony shad,
Big-bellied alewives, mackerels richly clad
With rainbow colors, the frost fish and the smelt,
As good as ever Lady Gustus[43] felt.
The spotted lamprons, eels, the lampreys
That seek fresh water brooks with Argus eyes;
These watery villagers with thousands more,
Do pass and repass near the verdant shore.

Kinds of all shellfish.

The luscious lobster, with the crabfish raw,
The brinish oyster, muscle, periwig,
And tortoise sought by the Indian's squaw,
Which to the flats dance many a winter jig,
To dive for cockles, and to dig for clams,
Whereby her lazy husband's guts she crams.[44]

To omit such of these as are not useful, therefore not to be spoken of, and only to certify you of such as be useful: first the seal, which is that which is called the sea calf. His skin is good for diverse uses. His body being between fish and flesh, it is not very delectable to the palate or congruent with the stomach. His oil is very good to burn in lamps, of which he affords a great deal. The shark is a kind of fish as big as a man, some as big as a horse, with three rows of teeth within his mouth, with

42. Obsolete variation of "seldom."
43. Wood was probably making a play on the word "gusty"—i. e., tasty or savory, from the Latin gustus.
44. For additional descriptions of New England waterlife see the two works by Josselyn cited in note 39 above.

which he snaps asunder the fisherman's lines if he be not very circumspect. This fish will leap at a man's hand if it be overboard and with his teeth snap off a man's leg or hand if he be a swimming. These are often taken, being good for nothing but to put on the ground for manuring of land.

The sturgeons be all over the country, but the best catching of them is upon the shoals of Cape Cod and in the river of Merrimac, where much is taken, pickled, and brought for England. Some of these be twelve, fourteen, eighteen foot long. I set not down the price of fish there because it is so cheap, so that one may have as much for two pence as would give him an angel in England. The salmon is as good as it is in England and in great plenty in some places. The halibut is not much unlike a plaice or turbot, some being two yards long and one wide and a foot thick; the plenty of better fish makes these of little esteem except the head and fins, which stewed or baked is very good. These halibuts be little set by while bass is in season. Thornback and skates is given to the dogs, being not counted worth the dressing in many places.

The bass is one of the best fishes in the country, and though men are soon wearied with other fish, yet are they never with bass; it is a delicate, fine, fat, fast fish, having a bone in his head which contains a saucerful of marrow, sweet and good, pleasant to the palate and wholesome to the stomach. When there be great store of them, we only eat the heads and salt up the bodies for winter, which exceeds ling or haberdine. Of these fishes some be three and some four foot long, some bigger, some lesser. At some tides a man may catch a dozen or twenty of these in three hours. The way to catch them is with hook and line: the fisherman taking a great cod-line, to which he fasteneth a piece of lobster and throws it into the sea, the fish biting at it he pulls her to him and knocks her on the head with a stick. These are at one time of the year (when alewives pass up the rivers) to be catched in rivers, in lobster time at the rocks, in mackerel time in the bays, at Michaelmas in the seas. When they use[d] to tide it in and out to the rivers and creeks, the English at the top of an high water do cross the creeks with long seines or bass nets which stop in the fish, and the water ebbing from them they are left on the dry ground, sometimes two or three thousand at a set, which are salted up against winter or distributed to such as have present occasion either to spend them in their houses or use them for their ground.

The herrings be much like them that be caught on the English coasts. Alewives be a kind of fish which is much like a herring, which in the latter end of April come up to the fresh rivers to spawn in such multitudes as is almost incredible, pressing up in such shallow waters as will scarce permit them to swim, having likewise such longing desire after the fresh water ponds that no beatings with poles or forcive agitations by other devices will cause them to return to the sea till they have cast their spawn. The shads be bigger than the English shads and fatter. The mackerels be of two sorts. In the beginning of the year are great ones, which be upon the coast; some are eighteen inches long. In summer—as in May, June, July, and August—come in a smaller kind of them. These mackerels are taken with drails which is a long small line with a lead and a hook at the end of it, being baited with a piece of red cloth. This kind of fish is counted a lean fish in England, but there it is so fat that it can scarce be saved against winter without reisting.[45] There be a great store of salt water eels, especially in such places where grass grows; for to take these there be certain eel pots made of osiers, which must be baited with a piece of lobster, into which the eels entering cannot return back again. Some take a bushel in a night in this manner, eating as many as they have need of for the present and salt up the rest against winter. These eels be not of so luscious a taste as they be in England, neither are they so aguish, but are both wholesome for the body and delightful for the taste. Lamprons and lampreys be not much set by.

Lobsters be in plenty in most places, very large ones, some being twenty pound in weight. These are taken at a low water amongst the rocks. They are very good fish, the small ones being the best; their plenty makes them little esteemed and seldom eaten. The Indians get many of them every day for to bait their hooks withal and to eat when they can get no bass. The oysters be great ones in form of a shoehorn; some be a foot long. These breed on certain banks that are bare every springtide. This fish without the shell is so big that it must admit of a division before you can well get it into your mouth. The periwig is a kind of fish that lieth in the ooze like a head of hair, which being touched conveys itself leaving nothing to be seen but a small round hole. Muscles be in great plenty, left only for the hogs, which if they were in England would be more esteemed of the poorer sort. Clams or clamps is a shellfish not

45. Obsolete form of "resting," itself an obsolete word for turning rancid.

much unlike a cockle; it lieth under the sand, every six or seven of them having a round hole to take air and receive water at. When the tide ebbs and flows, a man running over these clam banks will presently be made all wet by their spouting of water out of those small holes. These fishes be in great plenty in most places of the country, which is a great commodity for the feeding of swine both in winter and summer; for being once used to those places, they will repair to them as duly every ebb as if they were driven to them by keepers. In some places of the country there be clams as big as a penny white loaf, which are great dainties amongst the natives and would be in good esteem amongst the English were it not for better fish.

CHAP. 10

Of the Several Plantations in Particular.

Having described the situation of the country in general, with all his commodities arising from land and sea, it may add to your content and satisfaction to be informed of the situation of every several plantation, with his conveniences, commodities, and discommodities, etc., where first I will begin with the outmost plantation in the patent to the southward, which is called Wessaguscus,[46] an Indian name. This as it is but a small village, yet it is very pleasant and healthful, very good ground, and is well timbered and hath good store of hay ground. It hath a very spacious harbor for shipping before the town, the salt water being navigable for boats and pinnaces two leagues. Here the inhabitants have good store of fish of all sorts, and swine, having acorns and clams at the time of year. Here is likewise an alewife river.

Three miles to the north of this is Mount Wollaston,[47] a very fertile soil, and a place very convenient for farmers' houses, there being great

46. In the margin of the early editions was printed "Whichaguscusset," one of the numerous spellings of the Indian place which was renamed Weymouth in the early 1630s. For a description of Massachusetts towns ca. 1654, see Edward Johnson, *Johnson's Wonder-Working Providence, 1628-1651* (ed. J. Franklin Jameson, New York, 1910). A few years later (ca. 1660) Samuel Maverick compiled "A Briefe Description of New England. . . ," Massachusetts Historical Society, *Proceedings,* 2d ser. 1 (1884-85), 231-249.
47. Now in Quincy.

store of plain ground without trees. Near this place is Massachusetts Fields, where the greatest sagamore in the country lived before the plague,[48] who caused it to be cleared for himself. The greatest inconvenience is that there is not very many springs, as in other places of the country, yet water may be had for digging. A second inconvenience is that boats cannot come in at a low water, nor ships ride near the shore.

Six mile[s] further to the north lieth Dorchester, which is the greatest town in New England (but I am informed that others equal it since I came away); well wooded and watered; very good arable grounds and hay ground, fair cornfields and pleasant gardens, with kitchen gardens. In this plantation is a great many cattle, as kine, goats, and swine. This plantation hath a reasonable harbor for ships. Here is no alewife river, which is a great inconvenience. The inhabitants of this town were the first that set upon the trade of fishing in the bay, who received so much fruit of their labors that they encouraged others to the same undertakings.

A mile from this town lieth Roxbury, which is a fair and handsome country town, the inhabitants of it being all very rich. This town lieth upon the main so that it is well wooded and watered, having a clear and fresh brook running through the town, up which although there come no alewives yet there is great store of smelts, and therefore it is called Smelt Brook.

A quarter of a mile to the north side of the town is another river called Stony River, upon which is built a water mill. Here is good ground for corn and meadow for cattle. Up westward from the town it is something rocky, whence it hath the name of Roxbury. The inhabitants have fair houses, store of cattle, impaled cornfields, and fruitful gardens. Here is no harbor for ships because the town is seated in the bottom of a shallow bay, which is made by the neck of land on which Boston is built, so that they can transport all their goods from the ships in boats from Boston, which is the nearest harbor.

Boston[49] is two miles northeast from Roxbury. His situation is very

48. Probably the smallpox epidemic of 1633. See John Winthrop, *Winthrop's Journal "History of New England," 1630-1649* (ed. James Kendall Hosmer, 2 vols., New York, 1908), 1, 114f.

49. The best modern study of the town and its inhabitants is Darrett B. Rutman, *Winthrop's Boston: Portrait of a Puritan Town* (Chapel Hill, N. C., 1965). On its physical expansion see Walter M. Whitehill, *Boston: A Topographical History* (Cambridge, Mass., 1959).

pleasant, being a peninsula hemmed in on the south side with the Bay of Roxbury, on the north side with Charles River, the marshes on the back side being not half a quarter of a mile over, so that a little fencing will secure their cattle from the wolves. Their greatest wants be wood and meadow ground, which never were in that place, being constrained to fetch their building timber and fire wood from the islands in boats, and their hay in loyters.[50] It being a neck and bare of wood, they are not troubled with three great annoyances of wolves, rattlesnakes, and mosquitoes. These that live here upon their cattle must be constrained to take farms in the country or else they cannot subsist, the place being too small to contain many and fittest for such as can trade into England for such commodities as the country wants, being the chief place for shipping and merchandize.

This neck of land is not above four miles in compass, in form almost square, having on the south side at one corner a great broad hill whereon is planted a fort which can command any ship as she sails into any harbor within the hill [still?] bay. On the north side is another hill, equal in bigness, whereon stands a windmill. To the northwest is an high mountain with three little rising hills on the top of it, wherefore it is called the Tremont. From the top of this mountain a man may overlook all the islands which lie before the bay, and descry such ships as are upon the seacoast. This town, although it be neither the greatest nor the richest, yet it is the most noted and frequented, being the center of the plantations where the monthly courts were kept. (This town is greater and richer since I came away, and the courts are now kept at Newtown.) Here likewise dwells the governor.[51] This place hath very good land, affording rich cornfields and fruitful gardens, having likewise sweet and pleasant springs. The inhabitants of this place for their enlargement have taken to themselves farm houses in a place called Muddy River,[52] two miles from their town, where is good ground, large timber, and store of marshland and meadow. In this place they keep their swine and other cattle in the summer, whilst the corn is on the ground at Boston, and bring them to the town in winter.

On the north side of Charles River is Charlestown, which is another neck of land on whose north side runs Mystic River. This town for all

50. Obsolete form of "lighter."
51. John Winthrop (1588–1649).
52. Now Brookline.

things may be well paralleled with her neighbor Boston, being in the same fashion with her bare neck and constrained to borrow conveniences from the main, and to provide for themselves farms in the country for their better subsistance. At this town there is kept a ferryboat to convey passengers over Charles River, which between the two towns is a quarter of a mile over, being a very deep channel. Here may ride forty ships at a time. Up higher it is a broad bay, being above two miles between the shores, into which runs Stony River and Muddy River.

Towards the southwest in the middle of this bay is a great oyster bank. Towards the northwest of this bay is a great creek upon whose shore is situated the village of Medford, a very fertile and pleasant place and fit for more inhabitants than are yet in it. This town is a mile and half from Charlestown and at the bottom of this bay the river begins to be narrower, being but half a quarter of a mile broad.

By the side of this river is built Newtown,[53] which is three miles by land from Charlestown and a league and a half by water. This place was first intended for a city, but upon more serious considerations it was not thought so fit, being too far from the sea being the greatest inconvenience it hath. This is one of the neatest and best compacted towns in New England, having many fair structures, with many handsome contrived streets. The inhabitants, most of them, are very rich and well stored with cattle of all sorts, having many hundred acres of ground paled in with one general fence which is about a mile and a half long, which secures all their weaker cattle from the wild beasts. On the other side of the river lieth all their meadow and marshground for hay.

Half a mile westward of this plantation is Watertown, a place nothing inferior for land, wood, meadow, and water to Newtown. Within half a mile of this town is a great pond, which is divided between those two towns, which divides their bounds northward. A mile and a half from this town is a fall of fresh waters which convey themselves into the ocean through Charles River. A little below this fall of waters the inhabitants of Watertown have built a weir to catch fish, wherein they take great store of shads and alewives. In two tides they have gotten one hundred thousand of those fishes. This is no small benefit to the plantation. Ships of small burden may come up to these two towns, but the oyster banks do bar out the bigger ships.

53. Renamed Cambridge in 1638 after the colony established its college there.

The next town is Mystic,[54] which is three miles from Charlestown by land and a league and a half by water. It is seated by the water's side very pleasantly; there be not many houses as yet. At the head of this river are great and spacious ponds, whither the alewives press to spawn. This being a noted place for that kind of fish, the English resort thither to take them. On the west side of this river the governor hath a farm where he keeps most of his cattle. On the east side is Master Cradock's plantation,[55] where he hath impaled a park where he keeps his cattle till he can store it with deer. Here likewise he is at charges of building ships. The last year one was upon the stocks of a hundred ton; that being finished, they are to build one twice her burden. Ships without either ballast or loading may float down this river; otherwise the oyster bank would hinder them which crosseth the channel.

The last town in the still bay is Winnisimet,[56] a very sweet place for situation and stands very commodiously, being fit to entertain more planters than are yet seated. It is within a mile of Charlestown, the river only parting them.

The chief islands[57] which keep out the wind and the sea from disturbing the harbors are first Deer Island, which lies within a flight-shot of Pullin Point. This island is so called because of the deer which often swim thither from the main when they are chased by the wolves. Some have killed sixteen deer in a day upon this island. The opposite shore is called Pullin Point because that is the usual channel boats use to pass through into the bay, and the tide being very strong they are constrained to go ashore and hale their boats by the seizing or roads, whereupon it was called Pullin Point. The next island of note is Long Island, so called from his longitude. Diverse other islands be within these: viz. Noddles Isle, Round Isle, the Governor's Garden, where is planted an orchard and a vineyard with many other conveniences; and Slate Island, Glass Island, Bird Island, etc.[58] These isles abound with woods and water and meadow ground, and whatsoever the spacious fertile main affords. The

54. Later incorporated into modern Medford; old Medford was absorbed into Charlestown.
55. Matthew Cradock, a leader in the Puritan group that obtained a charter for Massachusetts, had a farm and shipyard in the colony but never migrated to America.
56. Renamed Chelsea.
57. In margin: "Islands there."
58. Some of these islands no longer exist; others are known by different names. See Alexander Young, ed., *Chronicles of the First Planters of the Colony of Mas-*

inhabitants use to put their cattle in these for safety, viz. their rams, goats, and swine, when their corn is on the ground.

Those towns that lie without the bay are a great deal nearer the main and reap a greater benefit from the sea in regard of the plenty both of fish and fowl which they receive from thence, so that they live more comfortably and at less charges than those that are more remote from the sea in the inland plantations.

The next plantation is Saugus,[59] six miles northeast from Winnisimet. This town is pleasant for situation, seated at the bottom of a bay which is made on the one side with the surrounding shore and on the other side with a long sandy beach which is two miles long at the end, whereon is a neck of land called Nahant. It is six miles in circumference, well wooded with oaks, pines, and cedars. It is beside well watered, having beside the fresh springs a great pond in the middle, before which is a spacious marsh. In this neck is store of good ground, fit for the plow, but for the present it is only used for to put young cattle in, and weather goats and swine to secure them from the wolves. A few posts and rails from the low water marks to the shore keeps out the wolves and keeps in the cattle. One Black William, an Indian duke, out of his generosity gave this place in general to this plantation of Saugus, so that no other can appropriate it to himself.

Upon the south side of the sandy beach the sea beateth, which is a true prognostication to presage storms and foul weather and the breaking up of the frost. For when a storm hath been, or is likely to be, it will roar like thunder, being heard six miles; and after storms [the sea] casts up great store of great clams which the Indians, taking out of their shells, carry out in baskets. On the north side of this bay is two great marshes which are made two by a pleasant river which runs between them. Northward up this river goes great store of alewives, of which they make good red herrings, in so much that they have been at charges to make a weir and a herringhouse to dry these herrings in; the last year were dried some four or five last for an experiment, which proved very good to appearance, if they prove as well in a foreign market. This is like to prove a great enrichment to the land (being a staple commodity in other countries) for there be such innumerable companies in every

---

sachusetts Bay (Boston, 1846), p. 405, n. 4, for their designations in the mid-nineteenth century.
59. Renamed Lynn.

river that I have seen ten thousand taken in two hours by two men without any weir at all, saving a few stones to stop their passage up the river. There likewise come store of bass which the Indians and English catch with hook and line, some fifty or threescore at a tide.

At the mouth of this river runs up a great creek into that great marsh, which is called Rumny Marsh,[60] which is four miles long and two miles broad, half of it being marsh ground and half upland grass without tree or bush. This marsh is crossed with diverse creeks, wherein lie great store of geese and ducks. There be convenient ponds for the planting of duck coys. Here is likewise belonging to this place diverse fresh meadows, which afford good grass, and four spacious ponds like little lakes, wherein is store of fresh fish within a mile of the town, out of which runs a curious fresh brook that is seldom frozen by reason of the warmness of the water. Upon this stream is built a water mill, and up this river comes smelts and frost fish much bigger than a gudgeon. For wood there is no want, there being store of good oaks, walnut, cedar, asp, elm. The ground is very good, in many places without trees, fit for the plow. In this plantation is more English tillage than in all New England and Virginia besides, which proved as well as could be expected, the corn being very good, especially the barley, rye, and oats.

The land affordeth the inhabitants as many rarities as any place else, and the sea more. The bass continuing from the middle of April to Michaelmas, which stays not above half that time in the bay, besides here is a great deal of rock-cod and mackerel, insomuch that shoals of bass have driven up shoals of mackerel from one end of the sandy beach to another, which the inhabitants have gathered up in wheelbarrows. The bay that lieth before the town at a low spring-tide will be all flats for two miles together, upon which is great store of muscle banks and clam banks, and lobsters amongst the rocks and grassy holes. These flats make it unnavigable for ships, yet at high water great boats, loyters,[61] and pinnaces of twenty and thirty ton, may sail up to the plantation. But they need have a skillful pilot because of many dangerous rocks and foaming breakers that lie at the mouth of that bay. The very aspect of the place is fortification enough to keep off an unknown enemy, yet may it be fortified at a little charge, being but few landing places thereabout and those obscure.

60. Now part of Chelsea.
61. See note 50 above.

Four miles northeast from Saugus lieth Salem,[62] which stands on the middle of a neck of land very pleasantly, having a south river on the one side and a north river on the other side. Upon this neck where the most of the houses stand is very bad and sandy ground, yet for seven years together it hath brought forth exceeding good corn by being fished but every third year; in some places is very good ground, and good timber, and diverse springs hard by the seaside. Here likewise is store of fish, as basses, eels, lobsters, clams, etc. Although their land be none of the best, yet beyond these rivers is a very good soil, where they have taken farms and get their hay and plant their corn. There they cross these rivers with small canoes which are made of whole pine trees, being about two foot and a half over, and twenty foot long. In these likewise they go afowling, sometimes two leagues to sea. There be more canoes in this town than in all the whole patent, every household having a water horse or two. This town wants an alewife river, which is a great inconvenience. It hath two good harbors, the one being called Winter, and the other Summer Harbors, which lieth within Derby's Fort, which place if it were well fortified might keep ships from landing of forces in any of those two places.

Marvill Head [i.e., Marblehead] is a place which lieth four miles full south from Salem and is a very convenient place for plantation, especially for such as will set upon the trade of fishing. There was made here a ship's loading of fish the last year, where still stands the stages and drying scaffolds. Here be good harbor for boats and safe riding for ships.

Agawam[63] is nine miles to the north from Salem, which is one of the most spacious places for a plantation; being near the sea, it aboundeth with fish and flesh of fowls and beasts, great meads and marshes and plain plowing grounds, many good rivers and harbors, and no rattlesnakes. In a word, it is the best place but one, in my judgment, which is Merrimac,[64] lying eight miles beyond it, where is a river twenty leagues navigable. All along the river side is fresh marshes, in some places three miles broad. In this river is sturgeon, salmon, and bass, and diverse other kinds of fish. To conclude, the country scarce affordeth that which this place cannot yield, so that these two places may contain twice as many

62. Earlier called by its Indian name *Naumkeag*. Wood probably lived there in 1629–1630 before the arrival of the Winthrop fleet greatly expanded the colony's population and prompted the founding of several other towns.
63. Renamed Ipswich.
64. Renamed Newbury.

people as are yet in New England, there being as yet scarce any inhabitants in these two spacious places. Three miles beyond the river of Merrimac is the outside of our patent for the Massachusetts Bay. These be all the towns that were begun when I came for England, which was the 15 of August 1633.

CHAP. 11

Of the Evils and Such Things as
Are Hurtful in the Plantation.

I have informed you of the country in general and of every plantation in particular, with their commodities and wherein one excelleth another. Now that I may be every way faithful to my readers in this work, I will as fully and truly relate to you what is evil and of most annoyance to the inhabitants.

First, those which bring most prejudice to their estates are the ravenous wolves, which destroy the weaker cattle, but of these you have heard before. That which is most injurious to the person and life of man is a rattlesnake, which is generally a yard and a half long, as thick in the middle as the small of a man's leg. She hath a yellow belly, her back being spotted with black, russet, yellow, and green colors placed like scales; at her tail is a rattle with which she makes a noise when she is molested or when she seeth any approach near her. Her neck seems to be no thicker than a man's thumb yet can she swallow a squirrel, having a great wide mouth, with teeth as sharp as needles wherewith she biteth such as tread upon her. Her poison lieth in her teeth, for she hath no sting. When any man is bitten by any of these creatures, the poison spreads so suddenly through the veins and so runs to the heart that in one hour it causeth death unless he hath the antidote to expel the poison, which is a root called snakeweed which must be champed, the spittle swallowed, and the root applied to the sore; this is present cure against that which would be present death without it. This weed is rank poison if it be taken by any man that is not bitten, unless it be physically compounded. Whosoever is bitten by these snakes his flesh becomes as spotted as a leper until he be perfectly cured. It is reported that if the party live that is bitten, the snake will die, and if the party die, the snake will live.

This is a most poisonous and dangerous creature, yet nothing so bad
as the report goes of him in England, for whereas he is said to kill a man
with his breath and that he can fly, there is no such matter, for he is
naturally the most sleepy and unnimble creature that lives, never offering to leap or bite any man if he be not trodden on first, and it is their
desire in hot weather to lie in paths where the sun may shine on them,
where they will sleep so soundly that I have known four men stride over
one of them and never awake her. Five or six men have been bitten by
them, which by using of snakeweed were all cured, never any yet losing
his life by them. Cows have been bitten, but being cut in diverse places
and this weed thrust into their flesh were cured. I never heard of any
beast that was yet lost by any of them, saving one mare. A small switch
will easily kill one of these snakes. In many places of the country there
be none of them, as at Plymouth, Newtown, Agawam, Nahant, etc. In
some places they will live on one side of the river, and swimming but
over the water, as soon as they be come into the woods, they turn up
their yellow bellies and die. Up into the country westward from the
plantations is a high hill, which is called Rattlesnake Hill, where there is
great store of these poisonous creatures. There be diverse other kind of
snakes, one whereof is a great long black snake, two yards in length,
which will glide through the woods very swiftly; these never do any hurt,
neither doth any other kind of snakes molest either man or beast. These
creatures in the winter time creep into clefts of rocks and into holes underground where they lie close till May or June.

Here likewise be great store of frogs, which in the spring do chirp and
whistle like a bird, and at the latter end of summer croak like our English frogs. Here be also toads which will climb the tops of high trees
where they will sit croaking to the wonderment of such as are not acquainted with them. I never saw any fleshworms or moles, but pismires
and spiders be there.

There are likewise troublesome flies. First there is a wild bee or wasp
which commonly guards the grape, building her cobweb habitation
amongst the leaves. Secondly a great green fly, not much unlike our
horseflies in England; they will nip so sore that they will fetch blood
either of man or beast and be most troublesome where most cattle be,
which brings them from out of the woods to the houses. This fly continues but for the month of June. The third is a gurnipper, which is a
small black fly no bigger than a flea; her biting causeth an itching upon

the hands or face, which provoketh scratching which is troublesome to some. This fly is busy but in close mornings or evenings and continues not above three weeks; the least wind or heat expels them. The fourth is a mosquito which is not unlike to our gnats in England.[65] In places where there is no thick woods or swamps there is none or very few. In new plantations they be troublesome for the first year, but the wood decaying they vanish. These flies cannot endure wind, heat, or cold, so that these are only troublesome in close thick weather and against rain. Many that be bitten will fall a scratching, whereupon their faces and hands swell. Others are never troubled with them at all. Those likewise that swell with their biting the first year never swell the second. For my own part, I have been troubled as much with them, or some like them, in the fen country of England as ever I was there. Here be the flies that are called chantharides, so much esteemed of surgeons, with diverse kinds of butterflies.

Thus have you heard of the worst of the country. But some peradventure may say no, and reply that they have heard that the people have been often driven to great wants and extremities. To which I answer, it is true that some have lived for a certain time with a little bread, other[s] without any, yet all this argues nothing against the country in itself, but condemns the folly and improvidence of such as would venture into so rude and unmanaged a country without so much provisions as should have comfortably maintained them in health and strength till by their labors they had brought the land to yield his fruit. I have myself heard some say that they heard it was a rich land, a brave country, but when they came there they could see nothing but a few canvas booths and old houses, supposing at the first to have found walled towns, fortifications, and corn fields, as if towns could have built themselves or corn fields have grown of themselves without the husbandry of man. These men, missing of their expectations, returned home and railed upon the country.

Others may object that of late time there hath been great want. I deny it not, but look to the original and tell me from whence it came. The root of their want sprung up in England, for many hundreds hearing of the plenty of the country were so much their own foes and country's hindrance as to come without provision, which made things both dear

65. In the margin: "Some call the small black fly the mosquito, and that which is like our English gnat a gurnipper, but generally the bigger is termed a mosquito."

and scant. Wherefore let none blame the country so much as condemn
the indiscreetness of such as will needs run themselves upon hardship.
And I dare further assure any that will carry provision enough for a year
and a half shall not need to fear want, if he or his agents be industrious
to manage his estate and affairs. And whereas many do disparage the
land, saying a man cannot live without labor, in that they more disparage and discredit themselves in giving the world occasion to take notice
of their dronish disposition that would live off the sweat of another
man's brows. Surely they were much deceived, or else ill informed, that
ventured thither in hope to live in plenty and idleness, both at a time.
And it is as much pity as he that can work and will not should eat, as it
is pity that he that would work and cannot should fast. I condemn not
such therefore as are now there and are not able to work; but I advise
for the future those men that are of weak constitutions to keep at home
if their estates cannot maintain servants. For all [in] New England must
be workers in some kind. And whereas it hath been formerly reported
that boys of ten or twelve years of age might do much more than get
their living, that cannot be, for he must have more than a boy's head and
no less than a man's strength that intends to live comfortably; and he
that hath understanding and industry, with a stock of an hundred pound,
shall live better there than he shall do here of twenty pound per annum.

But many will say if it be thus, how comes it to pass then that they are
so poor? I answer, that they are poor but in comparison; compare them
with the rich merchants or great landed men in England and then I
know they will seem poor. There is no probability they should be exceeding rich, because none of such great estate went over yet. Besides,
a man of estate must first scatter before he gather; he must lay out mon-
ies for transporting of servants and cattle and goods, for houses and
fences and gardens, etc. This may make his purse seem light and to the
eye of others seem a leaking in his estate, whereas these disbursements
are for his future enrichments, for he being once well seated and quietly
settled his increase comes in double.

And howsoever they are accounted poor, they are well contented and
look not so much at abundance as at competency. So little is the poverty of the country that I am persuaded if many in England which are
constrained to beg their bread were there, they would live better than
many do here that have money to buy it. Furthermore, when corn is
scarce yet may they have either fish or flesh for their labor. And surely

that place is not miserably poor to them that are there, where four eggs may be had for a penny and a quart of new milk at the same rate; where butter is six pence a pound and cheshire cheese at five pence. Sure Middlesex affords London no better penny-worths. What though there be no such plenty as to cry these things in the streets? Yet every day affords these penny-worths to those that need them in most places. I dare not say in all. Can they be very poor where for four thousand souls there are fifteen hundred head of cattle, besides four thousand goats and swine innumerable? In an ill sheep year I have known mutton as dear in old England and dearer than goat's flesh is in New England, which is altogether as good if fancy be set aside.

CHAP. 12

What Provision is To Be Made for a Journey
at Sea, and What to Carry with Us for Our
Use at Land.

Many peradventure at the looking over of these relations may have inclinations or resolution for the voyage, to whom I wish all prosperity in their undertakings. Although I will use no forcive arguments to persuade any, but leave them to the relation, yet by way of advice I would commend to them a few lines from the pen of experience. And because the way to New England is over sea, it will not be amiss to give you directions what is necessary to be carried. Many, I suppose, know as well or better than myself, yet all do not; to those my directions tend.

Although every man have ship provisions allowed him for his five pound a man—which is salt beef, pork, salt fish, butter, cheese, peas, pottage, water gruel, and such kind of victuals, with good biscuits, and six-shilling beer—yet will it be necessary to carry some comfortable refreshing of fresh victual. As first, for such as have ability, some conserves, and good claret wine to burn at sea. Or you may have it by some of your vintners or wine coopers burned here and put up into vessels which will keep much better than other burnt wine. It is a very comfortable thing for the stomach or such as are seasick. Salad oil likewise. Prunes are good to be stewed; sugar for many things. White biscuits and eggs, and bacon, rice, poultry, and some weather sheep to kill aboard the ship;

and fine flour-baked meats will keep about a week or nine days at sea. Juice of lemons well put up is good either to prevent or cure the scurvy.

Here it must not be forgotten to carry small skillets or pipkins, and small frying pans to dress their victuals in at sea. For bedding, so it be easy and cleanly and warm, it is no matter how old or coarse it be for the use of the sea; and so likewise for apparel, the oldest clothes be the fittest, with a long coarse coat to keep better things from the pitched ropes and planks. Whosoever shall put to sea in a stout and well-conditioned ship, having an honest master and loving seamen, shall not need to fear but he shall find as good content at sea as at land. It is too common with many to fear the sea more than they need, and all such as put to sea confesses it to be less tedious than they either feared or expected. A ship at sea may well be compared to a cradle rocked by a careful mother's hand, which though it be moved up and down is it not in danger of falling. So a ship may often be rocked too and again upon the troublesome sea, yet seldom doth it sink or overturn because it is kept by that careful hand of Providence by which it is rocked. It was never known yet that any ship in that voyage was cast away, or that ever fell into the enemy's hand.

For the health of passengers, it hath been observed that of six hundred souls not above three or four have died at sea. It is probable in such a company more might have died either by sickness or casualties if they had stayed at home. For women, I see not but that they do as well as men, and young children as well as either, having their healths as well at sea as at land. Many likewise which have come with such foul bodies to sea as did make their days uncomfortable at land have been so purged and clarified at sea that they have been more healthful for aftertimes, their weak appetites being turned to good stomachs, not only desiring but likewise digesting such victuals as the sea affords.

Secondly, for directions for the country, it is not to be feared but that men of good estates may do well there, always provided that they go well accommodated with servants. In which I would not wish them to take over-many, ten or twelve lusty servants being able to manage an estate of two or three thousand pound. It is not the multiplicity of many bad servants (which presently eats a man out of house and harbor, as lamentable experience hath made manifest), but the industry of the faithful and diligent laborer that enricheth the careful master; so that he that hath many dronish servants shall soon be poor and he that hath an industrious family shall as soon be rich.

Now, for the encouragement of his men he must not do as many have done (more through ignorance than desire): carry many mouths and no meat, but rather much meat for a few mouths. Want of due maintenance produceth nothing but a grumbling spirit with a sluggish idleness, whenas those servants which be well provided for go through their employments with speed and cheerfulness. For meal, it will be requisite to carry a hogshead and a half for everyone that is a laborer to keep him till he may receive the fruit of his own labors, which will be a year and a half after his arrival if he land in May or June. He must likewise carry malt, beef, butter, cheese, some peas, good wines, vinegar, strong waters, etc. Whosoever transports more of these than he himself useth, his overplus being sold will yield as much profit as any other staple commodity. Every man likewise must carry over good store of apparel; for if he come to buy it there, he shall find it dearer than in England. Woolen cloth is a very good commodity and linen better, as holland, lockram, flaxen, hempen, calico stuffs, linsey-woolseys, and blue calico, green sayes[66] for housewives' aprons, hats, boots, shoes, good Irish stockings, which if they be good are much more serviceable than knit ones. All kinds of grocery wares, as sugar, prunes, raisins, currants, honey, nutmegs, cloves, etc., soap, candles and lamps, etc.

All manner of household stuff is very good trade there, as pewter and brass, but great iron pots be preferred before brass for the use of that country. Warming pans and stewing pans be of necessary use and good traffic there. All manner of ironwares, as all manner of nails for houses and all manner of spikes for building of boats, ships, and fishing stages. All manner of tools for workmen, hoes for planters, broad and narrow for setting and weeding; with axes, both broad and pitching axes. All manner of augers, piercing bits, whipsaws, two-handed saws, froes, both for the riving of pales and laths, rings for beetles heads, and iron wedges. Though all these be made in the country (there being diverse blacksmiths), yet being a heavy commodity and taking but a little stowage it is cheaper to carry such commodities out of England. Glass ought not to be forgotten of any that desire to benefit themselves or the country. If it be well leaded and carefully packed up, I know no commodity bet-

66. A fine-textured cloth used for clothing.

ter for portage or sale. Here likewise must not be forgotten all utensils for the sea, as barbels, splitting knives, leads, and cod hooks and lines, mackerel hooks and lines, shark hooks, seines or bass nets, large and strong, herring nets, etc. Such as would eat fowl must not forget their six-foot guns, their good powder and shot of all sorts; a great round shot called bastable shot is the best, being made of a blacker lead than ordinary shot. Furthermore, good poldavies[67] to make sails for boats, roads and anchors for boats and pinnaces be good; sea-coal, iron, lead, and millstones, flints, ordnances, and whatsoever a man can conceive is good for the country that will lie as ballast he cannot be a loser by it.

And lest I should forget a thing of so great importance, no man must neglect to provide for himself, or those belonging to him, his munition for the defense of himself and the country. For there is no man there that bears a head but that bears military arms. Even boys of fourteen years of age are practiced with men in military discipline every three weeks. Whosoever shall carry over drums and English colors, partisans, halberds, pikes, muskets, bandoleers with swords, shall not need to fear good gain for them, such things being wanting in the country. Likewise, whatsoever shall be needful for fortifications of holds and castles, whereby the common enemy may be kept out in future times, is much desired. They as yet have had no great cause to fear, but because security hath been the overthrow of many a new plantation it is their care, according to their abilities, to secure themselves by fortifications as well as they can.[68]

Thus having showed what commodities are most useful, it will not be amiss to show you what men be most fit for these plantations. First, men of good working and contriving heads, a well experienced commonwealth's man for the good of the body politic in matters of advice and counsel; a well-skilled and industrious husbandman for tillage and improvements of grounds; an ingenious carpenter, a cunning joiner, a handy cooper, such a one as can make strong ware for the use of the coun-

67. Coarse canvas or sacking.
68. On colonial weaponry see Harold L. Peterson, *Arms and Armor in Colonial America, 1526–1783* (New York, 1956). On early New England militia practices see Douglas Edward Leach, "The Military System of Plymouth Colony," *New England Quarterly* 34 (1951), 342–364; H. Telfer Mook, "Training Day in New England," *New England Quarterly,* 11 (1938), 675–697; and Allen French, "Arms and Military Training of Our Colonizing Ancestors," Massachusetts Historical Society, *Proceedings* 67 (1945), 3-21.

try, and a good brick-maker, a tiler and a smith, a leather dresser, a gardener, and a tailor. One that hath good skill in the trade of fishing is of special use, and so is a good fowler; if there be any that hath skill in any of these trades, if he can transport himself, he needs not fear but he may improve his time and endeavors to his own benefit and comfort. If any cannot transport himself, he may provide himself of an honest master and so may do as well. There is as much freedom and liberty for servants as in England and more too; a wronged servant shall have right *volens nolens*[69] from his injurious master, and a wronged master shall have right of his injurious servant as well as here. Wherefore let no servant be discouraged from the voyage that intends it.

And now whereas it is generally reported that servants and poor men grow rich, and the masters and gentry grow poor, I must needs confess that the diligent hand makes rich and that laboring men having good store of employments, and as good pay, live well and contentedly. But I cannot perceive that those that set them awork are any way impoverished by them; peradventure they have less money by reason of them, but never the less riches, a man's work well done being more beneficial than his money or other dead commodities which otherwise would lie by him to no purpose. If any men be so improvident as to set men about building of castles in the air, or other unnecessary employments, they may grow poor; but such as employ laborers about planting of corn, building of houses, fencing in of ground, fishing, and diverse other necessary occasions, shall receive as much or more by poor men's labors than those that live in England do from the industry of such as they hire. Wherefore I do suppose this to be but the surmisings of some that are ignorant of the state of the country, or else misinformed by some ill-willers to the plantations.

Many objections I know are daily invented to hinder the proceedings of these new plantations, which may damp the unsettled spirits of such as are not greatly affected with those undertakings. Some say the Spaniard lays claim to the whole country, being the first discoverer hereof, and that he may make invasion upon those parts as well as he hath done upon St. Christophers and St. Martins and those places. But it doth not follow that because he took such places as lay just in his way to the West Indies that he should come thousands of miles with a great navy to plantations as yet not worth the pillage. And when the plantations are

69. Transl.: "Wishing, not wishing," or more loosely, "willy-nilly."

grown noted in the eyes of the common foes for wealth, it is hoped that when the bees have honey in their hives they will have stings in their tails. Hath not Virginia been planted many years, which is four hundred miles nearer the Spaniard's course, and yet never met with any affrontments; so that this scruple smells of fear and pusillanimity.

To wipe away all groundless calumniations, and to answer to every too, too curious objectións and frivolous questions (some so simple as not ashamed to ask whether the sun shines there or no) were to run in *infinitum*; but I hope that the several manuscripts and letters and informations by word of mouth from some of our honest countrymen, which daily have recourse unto us, have given full satisfaction to such as are well-willers to the plantations. And for such as are estranged to it in affection, if every word that hath been either writ or spoken were a forcive argument, yet would it be too little to steady their belief in any one particular concerning the country. Some are nimble-eared to hear faults, and so ready-tongued to publish them, yea oftentimes with strained constructions; a false asseveration usually winneth more belief than two verifying negatives can resettle. Some there are who count with Claudian that it is an incomparable happiness to have their birth, life, and burial in the same place; these are never likely to remove further than the shell of their own country. But because there are some noble spirits that devote their states, and their persons, to the common good of their king and country, I have therefore for their direction and delight made this relation. For as the end of my travel was observation, so I desire the end of my observation may tend to the information of others. As I have observed what I have seen and written what I have observed, so do I desire to publish what I have written, desiring it may be beneficial to posterity; and if any man desire to fill himself at that fountain from whence this tasting cup was taken, his own experience shall tell him as much as I have here related. And thus I pass from the country as it stands to the English and come to discourse how it stands to the old natives, and they to it, as followeth.

The Second Part

Of the Indians, Their Persons, Clothings, Diet, Natures,
Customs, Laws, Marriages, Worships, Conjurations, Wars,
Games, Huntings, Fishings, Sports, Language, Death, and Burials.

CHAP. 1

Of the Connecticuts, Mohawks, or Such Indians
as Are Westward.

The country as it is in relation to the Indians is divided, as it were, into shires, every several division being swayed by a several king. The Indians to the east and northeast, bearing the name of Churchers and Tarrenteens; these in the southern parts be called Pequots and Narragansetts; those who are seated westward be called Connecticuts and Mohawks. Our Indians that live to the northward of them be called Aberginians, who before the sweeping plague were an inhabitant not fearing, but rather scorning, the confrontments of such as now count them but the scum of the country and would soon root them out of their native possessions were it not for the English.[1]

These [Mohawks] are a cruel bloody people which were wont to come

1. With the exception of the Mohawks, the tribes mentioned in this paragraph and described below belonged to the Algonquian linguistic stock. They lived along the Atlantic littoral, from northern Maine to southern Connecticut. The Mohawks, easternmost tribe of the Iroquois Confederacy (and of Iroquoian linguistic stock), lived near Albany, New York. For another seventeenth century description of these tribes—and of some Wood neglected—see Daniel Gookin, *Historical Collections of the Indians in New England* (Boston, 1792; repr. New York, 1972), chap. IV. For a more modern assessment see Frederick Webb Hodge, ed., *Handbook of American Indians North of Mexico* (Washington, D. C., 1907; repr. New York, 1959).

down upon their poor neighbors with more than brutish savageness,
spoiling their corn, burning their houses, slaying men, ravishing women;
yea very cannibals they were, sometimes eating on a man, one part after
another, before his face and while yet living, in so much that the very
name of a Mohawk would strike the heart of a poor Aberginian dead,
were there not hopes at hand of relief from the English to succor them.[2]
For these inhuman homicides confess that they dare not meddle with a
white-faced man, accompanied with his hot-mouthed weapon. These Indians be a people of a tall stature, of long grim visages, slender waisted,
and exceeding great arms and thighs, wherein they say their strength
lieth; and this I rather believe because an honest gentleman told me, upon his knowledge, that he saw one of them with a fillip with his finger
kill a dog, who afterward flead[3] him and sod[4] him, and eat him to his
dinner. They are so hardy that they can eat such things as would make
other Indians sick to look upon.

Being destitute of fish and flesh, they suffice hunger and maintain nature with the use of vegetatives. But that which they most hunt after is
the flesh of man; their custom is if they get a stranger near their habitations not to butcher him immediately, but keeping him in as good plight
as they can, feeding him with the best victuals they have. As a near-
neighboring Indian assured me, who found what he had spoke true by a
lamentable experience (still wearing the cognizance of their cruelty on
his naked arm) who being taken by them, eat of their food [and] lodged
in their beds, nay he was brought forth every day to be new painted,
piped unto, and hemmed in with a ring of bare-skinned morris dancers,[5]
who presented their antics before him. In a word, when they had sport-
ed enough about this walking Maypole, a rough-hewn satyr cutteth a
gobbit of flesh from his brawny arm, eating it in his view, searing it with
a fire-brand lest the blood should be wasted before the morning, at the
dawning whereof they told him they would make an end as they had
begun. He answered that he cared as little for their threats as they did

2. As traditional enemies of the New England tribes, the Mohawks gained a reputation for brutality and cannibalism that was at least partly based on fact. However, Mohawk cannibalism was ceremonial rather than dietary, and Mohawk
ferocity was probably no greater than that of several other eastern tribes, as Wood
himself reveals in his description of the Tarrantines.
3. Obsolete form of flay.
4. Obsolete form of seethe—i.e., to boil.
5. I.e., grotesque dancers or performers.

for his life, not fearing death; whereupon they led him bound into a wigwam where he sat as a condemned prisoner, grating his teeth for anger,
being for the present so hampered and the next day to be entombed in
so many living sepulchers. He extends his strength to the utmost, break-
eth the bands from his hands and loosing the cords from his feet, thought
at once to be revenged for the flesh of his arm, and finding a hatchet
lays on with an arm of revenge to the unliving of ten men at first onset.
Afterward taking the opportunity of the dead of the night, [he] fled
through the woods and came to his native home where he still lives to
rehearse his happy escapal. Of the rest of their inhuman cruelties let
the Dutchmen (who live among them) testify, as likewise the cruel manner of leading their prisoners captive, whom they do not only pinion
with sharp thongs but likewise bore holes through their hamstrings,
through which they thread a cord coupling ten or a dozen men together.[6]

These Indians be more desperate in wars than the other Indians, which
proceeds not only from the fierceness of their natures but also in that
they know themselves to be better armed and weaponed, all of them
wearing sea horse skins and barks of trees (made by their art as impenetrable, it is thought, as steel), wearing head pieces of the same, under
which they march securely and undauntedly, running and fiercely crying out *"Hadree Hadree succomee succomee"* (we come, we come to
suck your blood), not fearing the feathered shafts of the strong-armed
bowmen, but like unruly headstrong stallions beat them down with
their right hand tomahawks and left hand javelins, being all the weapons
which they use, counting bows a cowardly fight. Tomahawks be staves
of two foot and a half long, and a knob at one end as round and big as
a football. A javelin is a short spear, headed with sharp sea horse teeth;
one blow or thrust with these strange weapons will not need a second
to hasten death from a Mohawk's arm.[7]

6. On Indian captivity and torture see Nathaniel Knowles, "The Torture of Cap-
tives by the Indians of Eastern North America," American Philosophical Society,
Proceedings, 82 (1940), 151–225; James Axtell, "The Scholastic Philosophy of the
Wilderness," *William and Mary Quarterly,* 3rd ser. 29 (1972), 335–366; and "The
White Indians of Colonial America," *ibid.,* 3rd ser. 32 (1975), 55-88.
7. On Indian warfare see Wendell S. Hadlock "War among the Northeastern Woodland Indians," *American Anthropologist,* new ser. 49 (1947), 204–221; Patrick
Malone, "Changing Military Technology among the Indians of Southern New Eng-
land," *American Quarterly,* 25 (1973), 48–63; and Francis Jennings, *The Invasion*

I will conclude this discourse concerning the Mohawks in a tragical re-
hearsal of one of their combats. A sagamore[8] inhabiting near these cannibals was so daily annoyed with their injurious inhumanity that he
must either become a tributary subject to their tyranny or release himself from thraldom by the stroke of war, which he was unable to wage
of himself. Wherefore with fair entreaties, plausible persuasions, forcive
arguments, and rich presents he sent to other sagamores, he procured so
many soldiers as, summed with his own, made his forces six thousand
strong; with the which he resolutely marched towards his enemies, in-
tending either to win the horse or lose the saddle. His enemies, having
heard of his designs, plotted how to confront him in his enterprise and
overthrow him by treachery, which they thus attempted: knowing their
enemies were to swim over a muddy river, they divided their bands, lying in ambush on both sides the river waiting his approach, who suspected no danger, looking for nothing but victory. But immediately they
were environed with their unexpected foes in their greatest disadvan-
tage, for being in the water, shoot they could not, for swimming was
their action. And when they came to the side, they could not run away,
for their feet stuck fast in the mud, and their adversaries impaled them
about, clubbing and darting all that attained the shore, so that all were
killed and captived saving three, who—swimming farther under the waters (like the duck that escapeth the spaniel by diving) until they were
out of sight of their bloodthirsty foes—recovered the shore, creeping into the thickets from whence after a little breathing and resting of their
weary limbs they marched through the woods and arrived at their own
homes, relating to their inquisitive survivors the sad event of their war,
who a long time after deplored the death of their friends, still placing
the remembrance of that day in the calendar of their mishaps.

---

of America: Indians, Colonialism, and the Cant of Conquest (Chapel Hill, N. C.,
1975), chap. IX. For the impact of hostilities on the Indian population see Sherburne F. Cook, "Interracial Warfare and Population Decline among New England
Indians," Ethnobistory, 20 (1973), 1–24.
8. "Sachem" and "sagamore" were interchangeable terms throughout most of
New England and were translated roughly into "chief."

CHAP. 2

Of the Tarranteens or the Indians
Inhabiting Eastward.

The Tarrenteens,[9] saving that they eat not man's flesh, are little less savage and cruel than these cannibals. Our Indians do fear them as their deadly enemies, for so many of them as they meet they kill. About two years ago, our Indians being busy about their accustomed huntings, not suspecting them so near their own liberties, were on the sudden surprised by them, some being slain, the rest escaping to their English asylum, whitehr they durst not pursue them. Their sagamore was wounded by presently cured by English surgery.

These Indians are the more insolent by reason they have guns which they daily trade for with the French, who will sell his eyes, as they say, for beaver. But these do them more credit than service; for having guns they want powder, or if they have that they want shot, something or other being always wanting; so that they use them for little but to salute coasting boats that come to trade, who no sooner can anchor in any harbor but they present them with a volley of shot, asking for sack and strong liquors which they so much love, since the English used to trade it with them, that they will scarce trade for anything else, lashing out into excessive abuse, first taught by the example of some of our English who to unclothe them of their beaver coat clad them with the infection of swearing and drinking, which was never in fashion with them before, it being contrary to their nature to guzzle down strong drink or use so much as to sip of strong-waters until our bestial example and dishonest incitation hath too much brought them to it.

From which I am sure hath sprung many evil consequents, as disorder, quarrels, wrongs, unconscionable and forcive wresting of beaver and wampompeag, and from overflowing cups there hath been a proceeding to revenge, murther, and overflowing of blood. As witness Master Way's boat, which they sunk with stones after they had killed his son, with three more, buzzing the English in the ears that they see it

9. Wood apparently referred to the Abnaki, a tribe inhabiting the valleys of the Kennebec, Androscoggin and Saco Rivers in Maine and adjacent New Hampshire. Because of the colder climate of their region, the Abnaki, unlike the tribes of southern New England, were primarily hunters rather than agriculturalists. See Hodge, *Handbook of American Indians,* 1, 5f, where the spelling is Tarrantines.

bulged against the rocks and the men drowned in the beating surges.[10] But afterwards, being betrayed, as many as were caught were hanged. Another who was situated on Richmond's Island, living as he list amongst them, making his covetous corrupt will his law, after many abuses was with his family one evening treacherously murthered under a fair pretence of trade; so that these that lived beside the law of God and their king, and the light of nature, died by their hands that cared neither for God, king, nor nature.[11]

Take these Indians in their own trim and natural disposition and they be reported to be wise, lofty-spirited, constant in friendship to one another, true in their promise, and more industrious than many others.

CHAP. 3

Of the Pequots and Narragansetts,
Indians Inhabiting Southward.

The Pequots[12] be a stately, warlike people, of whom I never heard any misdemeanor, but that they were just and equal in their dealings, not treacherous either to their countrymen or English, requiters of courtesies, affable towards the English.

Their next neighbors, the Narragansetts,[13] be at this present the most

10. See John Winthrop, *Winthrop's Journal, "History of New England," 1630–1649* (ed. James Kendall Hosmer, 2 vols., New York, 1908), 1, 82, for details on Henry Way of Dorchester who was killed, presumably by "the eastern Indians," in the winter of 1631-32.

11. See *Winthrop's Journal,* 1, 69, for details.

12. The Pequots had originally been part of the Mahican tribe of the upper Hudson River Valley. Sometime in the late sixteenth or early seventeenth century they moved into the lower Connecticut River region where they gained a reputation for belligerency with both Indians and Europeans. Although Wood seems to have been unaware of that reputation, his observation on the Pequots' opinion of the Narragansetts suggests that the Pequots were relatively martial. In 1637 the Pequots were crushed by the New England colonies in the first major clash between settlers and Indians. For other descriptions of the tribe see Gookin, *Historical Collections,* p. 7; and John W. DeForest, *History of the Indians of Connecticut from the Earliest Known Period to 1850* (Hartford, 1852), passim.

13. The Narragansetts controlled the area from Narragansett Bay on the east to the Pawcatuck River on the west. Despite their relatively unmartial demeanor, the Narragansetts were usually safe from attacks by other tribes because of their num-

numerous people in those parts, the most rich also, and the most industrious, being the storehouse of all such kind of wild merchandise as is amongst them. These men are the most curious minters of their wampompeag and mowhacheis, which they form out of the inmost wreaths of periwinkle shells.[14] The northern, eastern, and western Indians fetch all their coin from these southern mintmasters. From hence they have most of their curious pendants and bracelets. From hence they have their great stone pipes, which will hold a quarter of an ounce of tobacco, which they make with steel drills and other instruments. Such is their ingenuity and dexterity that they can imitate the English mold so accurately that were it not for matter and color it were hard to distinguish them. They make them of green and sometimes of black stone; they be much desired of our English tobacconists for their rarity, strength, handsomeness, and coolness. Hence likewise our Indians had their pots, wherein they used to seethe their victuals before they knew the use of brass. Since the English came, they have employed most of their time in catching of beavers, otters, and musquashes, which they bring down into the bay, returning back loaded with English commodities, of which they make a double profit by selling them to more remote Indians who are ignorant at what cheap rates they obtain them in comparison of what they make them pay, so making their neighbors' ignorance their enrichment. Although these be populous, yet I never heard they were desirous to take in hand any martial enterprise or expose themselves to the uncertain events of war, wherefore the Pequots call them women-like men. But being uncapable of a jeer, they rest secure under the conceit of their popularity and seek rather to grow rich by industry than famous by deeds of chivalry. But to leave strangers and come to declare what is experimentally known of the Indians amongst whom we live—of whom in the next chapter.

---

bers—about 4,000—which made them the largest tribe in New England. See Gookin, *Historical Collections,* pp. 7–10; and Hodge, *Handbook,* 2, 28–30.
14. For more extensive discussions of wampum see Gookin, *Historical Collections,* pp. 17–18; Frank G. Speck, "The Functions of Wampum among the Eastern Algonkian," American Anthropological Society, *Memoirs,* 6 (1919), 3–71; Alden T. Vaughan, *New England Frontier: Puritans and Indians, 1620–1675* (Boston, 1965), pp. 20–24; and Wilbur Jacobs, *Dispossessing the American Indian* (New York, 1972), chap. 3.

CHAP. 4

Of the Aberginians or Indians Northward.[15]

First of their stature, most of them being between five or six foot high, straight bodied, strongly composed, smooth-skinned, merry countenanced, of complexion something more swarthy than Spaniards, black haired, high foreheaded, black eyed, out-nosed, broad shouldered, brawny armed, long and slender handed, out breasted, small waisted, lank bellied, well thighed, flat kneed, handsome grown legs, and small feet. In a word, take them when the blood brisks in their veins, when the flesh is on their backs and marrow in their bones, when they frolic in their antic deportments and Indian postures, and they are more amiable to behold (though only in Adam's livery) than many a compounded fantastic in the newest fashion.

It may puzzle belief to conceive how such lusty bodies should have their rise and daily supportment from so slender a fostering, their houses being mean, their lodging as homely, commons scant, their drink water, and nature their best clothing. In them the old proverb may well be verified: *Natura paucis contenta,*[16] for though this be their daily portion, they still are healthful and lusty. I have been in many places, yet did I never see one that was born either in redundance or defect a monster, or any that sickness had deformed, or casualty made decrepit, saving one that had a bleared eye and another that had a wen on his cheek. The reason is rendered why they grow so proportionable and continue so long in their vigor (most of them being fifty before a wrinkled brow or gray hair bewray their age) is because they are not brought down with suppressing labor, vexed with annoying cares, or drowned in the excessive abuse of overflowing plenty, which oftentimes kills them more than want, as may appear in them. For when they change their bare Indian commons for the plenty of England's fuller diet, it is so contrary to their stomachs that death or a desperate sickness immediately accrues, which makes so few of them desirous to see England.

15. Wood's term for the Indians north of Massachusetts Bay was not used by other early chroniclers or by subsequent authorities on the New England tribes. He apparently used "Aberginians" to mean, collectively, the Pennacooks, Passaconaways, and other tribes in northern Massachusetts and southern New Hampshire. See Hodge, *Handbook,* 1, 1.
16. Transl.: "Nature is satisfied with a few things."

Their swarthiness is the sun's livery, for they are born fair.[17] Their smooth skins proceed from the often annointing of their bodies with the oil of fishes and the fat of eagles, with the grease of raccoons, which they hold in summer the best antidote to keep their skin from blistering with the scorching sun, and it is their best armor against the mosquitoes, the surest expeller of the hairy excrement, and stops the pores of their bodies against the nipping winter's cold.

Their black hair is natural, yet it is brought to a more jetty color by oiling, dyeing, and daily dressing. Sometimes they wear it very long, hanging down in a loose, disheveled, womanish manner; otherwhile tied up hard and short like a horse tail, bound close with a fillet, which they say makes it grow the faster. They are not a little fantastical or customsick in this particular, their boys being not permitted to wear their hair long till sixteen years of age, and then they must come to it by degrees, some being cut with a long foretop, a long lock on the crown, one of each side of his head, the rest of his hair being cut even with the scalp. The young men and soldiers wear their hair long on the one side, the other side being cut short like a screw. Other cuts they have as their fancy befools them, which would torture the wits of a curious barber to imitate. But though they be thus wedded to the hair of their head, you cannot woo them to wear it on their chins, where it no sooner grows but it is stubbed up by the roots, for they count it as an unuseful, cumbersome, and opprobrious excrement, insomuch as they call him an Englishman's bastard that hath but the appearance of a beard, which some have growing in a staring fashion like the beard of a cat, which makes them the more out of love with them, choosing rather to have no beards than such as should make them ridiculous.

17. Seventeenth-century European commentators described Indian skin color as white or tawny, never as red. The concept of "Red Indians" appeared in the eighteenth century, initially in reference to red war paint.

CHAP. 5

Of Their Apparel, Ornaments, Paintings,
and Other Artificial Deckings.

Now these naked bodies may seem too weak to withstand the assaulting heat of their parching summers and the piercing cold of the icy winters. Or it may be surmised that these earthly fabrics should be wasted to nothing by the tempestuous dashings of wind-driven rains, having neither that which may warm within or shelter without. Yet these things they look not after, saving a pair of Indian breeches to cover that which modesty commands to be hid, which is but a piece of cloth a yard and a half long, put between their groinings, tied with a snake's skin about their middles, one end hanging down with a flap before, the other like a tail behind. In the wintertime the more aged of them wear leather drawers, in form like Irish trousers, fastened under their girdle with buttons. They wear shoes likewise of their own making, cut out of a moose's hide. Many of them wear skins about them, in form of an Irish mantle, and of these some be bear's skins, moose's skins, and beaver skins sewed together, otter skins, and raccoon skins; most of them in the winter having his deep-furred cat skin, like a long large muff, which he shifts to that arm which lieth most exposed to the wind. Thus clad, he bustles better through a world of cold in a frost-paved wilderness than the furred citizen in his warmer stove.

If their fancy drive them to trade, they choose rather a good coarse blanket, through which they cannot see, interposing it between the sun and them; or a piece of broad cloth, which they use for a double end, making it a coat by day and a covering by night. They love not to be imprisoned in our English fashion. They love their own dog fashion better (of shaking their ears and being ready in a moment) than to spend time in dressing them, though they may as well spare it as any men I know, having little else to do. But the chief reasons they render why they will not conform to our English apparel are because their women cannot wash them when they be soiled, and their means will not reach to buy new when they have done with their old. and they confidently believe the English will not be so liberal as to furnish them upon gifture. Therefore they had rather go naked than be lousy and bring their bodies out of their old tune, making them more tender by a new acquired habit which poverty would constrain them to leave.[18]

18. For other seventeenth-century descriptions of Indian apparel see James Rosier,

Although they be thus poor, yet is there in them the sparks of natural pride which appears in their longing desire after many kind[s] of ornaments, wearing pendants in their ears, as forms of birds, beasts, and fishes, carved out of bone, shells, and stone, with long bracelets of their curious wrought wamponipeag and mowhacheis which they put about their loins.[19] These they count a rare kind of decking, many of the better sort bearing upon their cheeks certain portraitures of beasts, as bears, deers, mooses, wolves, etc.; some of fowls, as of eagles, hawks, etc., which be not a superficial painting but a certain incision, or else a raising of their skin by a small sharp instrument under which they convey a certain kind of black unchangeable ink which makes the desired form apparent and permanent. Others have certain round impressions down the outside of their arms and breasts in form of mullets or spur-rowels,[20] which they imprint by searing irons. Whether these be foils to illustrate their unparalleled beauty (as they deem it) or arms to blazon their antique gentility, I cannot easily determine. But a sagamore with a humbird in his ear for a pendant, a black hawk on his occiput for his plume, mowhacheis for his gold chain, good store of wampompeag begirting his loins, his bow in his hand, his quiver at his back, with six naked Indian spatterlashes[21] at his heels for his guard, thinks himself little inferior to the great Cham. He will not stick to say he is all one with King Charles. He thinks he can blow down castles with his breath and conquer kingdoms with his conceit. This Pompey can endure no equal till one day's adverse lottery at their game (called puim) metamorphise him into a Codrus,[22] robbing him of his conceited wealth, leaving him in mind and riches equal with his naked attendants, till a new taxation furnish him with a fresh supply.

"A True Relation of the Voyage of Captaine George Waymouth, 1605," in Henry S. Burrage, ed., *Early English and French Voyages* (New York, 1906), pp. 368, 373; Thomas Morton, *New English Canaan* (Amsterdam, 1637; repr. New York, 1972), pp. 28–31; Roger Williams, *A Key into the Language of America* ed. by John J. Teunissen and Evelyn J. Hinz (Detroit, 1973), chap. 20; and Gookin, *Historical Collections,* p. 17.

19. The 1634 edition of *New England's Prospect* included "necks and" before "loins." For reasons nowhere explained, Wood omitted the reference to necks in the 1635 and 1639 editions, although many of his contemporaries noted that wampum was often worn as a necklace.

20. I.e., the rowel or pointed wheel on a rider's spur.

21. A variant spelling of "spatterdash"—a kind of legging worn to protect trousers from spatter. Here used figuratively.

22. According to Juvenal, Codrus was bequeathed considerable wealth but lost it all.

CHAP. 6

Of Their Diet, Cookery, Mealtimes, and
Hospitality at Their Kettles.

Having done with their most needful clothings and ornamental deckings, may it please you to feast your eyes with their belly-timbers, which I suppose would be but stibium[23] to weak stomachs as they cook it, though never so good of itself. In wintertime they have all manner of fowls of the water and of the land, and beasts of the land and water, pond-fish, with catharres and other roots, Indian beans, and clams. In the summer they have all manner of seafish, with all sorts of berries.[24]

For the ordering of their victuals, they boil or roast them, having large kettles which they traded for with the French long since, and do still buy of the English as their need requires. Before they had substantial earthern pots of their own making. Their spits are no other than cloven sticks, sharped at one end to thrust into the ground; into these cloven sticks they thrust the flesh or fish they would have roasted, behemming a round fire with a dozen spits at a time, turning them as they see occasion. Some of their scullery having dressed these homely cates, presents it to his guests, dishing it up in a rude manner, placing it on the verdant carpet of the earth which nature spreads them, without either trenchers, napkins, or knives, upon which their hunger-sauced stomachs, impatient of delays, falls aboard without scrupling at unwashed hands, without bread, salt, or beer, lolling on the Turkish fashion, not ceasing till their full bellies leave nothing but empty platters.

They seldom or never make bread of their Indian corn, but seethe it whole like beans, eating three or four corns with a mouthful of fish or flesh, sometimes eating meat first and corns after, filling up the chinks with their broth. In summer, when their corn is spent, isquoutersquash-

23. A form of antimony used as a poison or emetic.
24. By "catharres" Wood probably meant catmint or catnip (*Nepta Cataria*), although botanists do not consider that herb to have been native to America. See John Gerard, *The Herball or General Historie of Plants* (London, 1597; repr. Amsterdam, 1974), p. 554; Ann Leighton, *Early American Gardens: "For Meate or Medicine"* (Boston, 1970), pp. 196, 269f.; and *Oxford English Dictionary* (13 vols.; Oxford, 1933), 11, 188. On the diet of New England Indians see Gookin, *Historical Collections,* p. 15; Williams, *Key into the Language,* chap. 2; and M.K. Bennett, "The Food Economy of the New England Indians, 1605–1675," *Journal of Political Economy,* 63 (1955), 369–397.

es[25] is their best bread, a fruit like a young pumpion. To say and to speak paradoxically, they be great eaters and yet little meat-men. When they visit our English, being invited to eat, they are very moderate, whether it be to show their manners or for shamefacedness I know not. But at home they will eat till their bellies stand forth,[26] ready to split with fullness, it being their fashion to eat all at some times and sometimes nothing at all in two or three days, wise providence being a stranger to their wilder ways. They be right infidels, neither caring for the morrow or providing for their own families, but as all are fellows at football, so they all meet friends at the kettle, saving their wives that dance a spaniel-like attendance at their backs for their bony fragments.

If their imperious occasions cause them to travel, the best of their victuals for their journey is nocake (as they call it), which is nothing but Indian corn parched in the hot ashes. The ashes being sifted from it, it is afterward beaten to powder and put into a long leathern bag, trussed at their back like a knapsack, out of which they take thrice three spoonfuls a day, dividing it into three meals. If it be in winter and snow be on the ground, they can eat when they please, stopping snow[27] after their dusty victuals, which otherwise would feed them little better than a Tyburn halter.[28] In summer they must stay till they meet with a spring or brook where they may have water to prevent the imminent danger of choking. With this strange viaticum they will travel four or five days together, with loads fitter for elephants than men. But though they can fare so hardily abroad, at home their chaps must walk night and day as long as they have it. They keep no set meals; their store being spent, they champ on the bit till they meet with fresh supplies, either from their own endeavors or their wives' industry, who trudge to the clambanks when all other means fail. Though they be sometimes scanted, yet are they as free as emperors, both to their countrymen and English, be he stranger or near acquaintance, counting it a great discourtesy not to eat of their high-conceited delicates and sup of their unoatmealed

25. See note 19 to Part One above.
26. The 1634 and 1635 editions read "fouth"; the 1639 edition substitutes "South." Wood probably intended fouth—i.e., fullness or plenty.
27. "Stopping" is here used in the obsolete sense of satisfying the appetite, in this case eating snow instead of water.
28. During the seventeenth century Tyburn was the place of public execution in Middlesex, England. Wood here implies that without some snow to wash it down, the Indians' food would serve them no better than the hangman.

broth, made thick with fishes, fowls, and beasts boiled all together, some remaining raw, the rest converted by over-much seething to a loathed mash, not half so good as Irish boniclapper.[29]

CHAP. 7

Of Their Dispositions and Good Qualifications, as
Friendship, Constancy, Truth, and Affability.

To enter into a serious discourse concerning the natural conditions of these Indians might procure admiration from the people of any civilized nations, in regard of their civility and good natures. If a tree may be judged by his fruit, and dispositions calculated by exterior actions, then may it be concluded that these Indians are of affable, courteous, and well-disposed natures, ready to communicate the best of their wealth to the mutual good of one another; and the less abundance they have to manifest their entire friendship, so much the more perspicuous is their love in that they are as willing to part with their mite in poverty as treasure in plenty. As he that kills a deer sends for his friends and eats it merrily, so he that receives but a piece of bread from an English hand parts it equally between himself and his comrades, and eats it lovingly. In a word, a friend can command his friend his house and whatsoever is his (saving his wife), and have it freely. And as they are love-linked thus in common courtesy, so are they no way sooner disjointed than by ingratitude, accounting an ungrateful person a double robber of a man, not only of his courtesy but of his thanks which he might receive of another for the same proffered or received kindness. Such is their love to one another that they cannot endure to see their countrymen wronged, but will stand stiffly in their defense, plead strongly in their behalf, and justify one another's integrities in any warrantable action.[30]

If it were possible to recount the courtesies they have showed the English since their first arrival in those parts, it would not only steady belief that they are a loving people, but also win the love of those that never saw them, and wipe off that needless fear that is too deeply rooted

29. Variant spelling of "bonnyclabber"—coagulated sour milk.
30. On Indian disposition and hospitality see Gookin, *Historical Collections,* p. 19; and Rosier, "True Relation," p. 376.

in the conceits of many who think them envious and of such rancorous and inhumane dispositions that they will one day make an end of their English inmates. The worst indeed may be surmised, but the English hitherto have had little cause to suspect them but rather to be convinced of their trustiness, seeing they have as yet been the disclosers of all such treacheries as have been practised by other Indians. And whereas once there was a proffer of an universal league amongst all the Indians in those parts, to the intent that they might all join in one united force to extirpate the English, our Indians refused the motion, replying they had rather be servants to the English, of whom they were confident to receive no harm and from whom they had received so many favors and assured good testimonies of their love, than equals with them who would cut their throats upon the least offence and make them the shambles of their cruelty. Furthermore, if any roving ships be upon the coasts and chance to harbor either eastward, northward, or southward in any unusual port, they will give us certain intelligence of her burthen and forces, describing their men either by language or features, which is a great privilege and no small advantage. Many ways hath their advice and endeavor been advantageous unto us, they being our first instructors for the planting of their Indian corn, by teaching us to cull out the finest seed, to observe the fittest season, to keep distance for holes and fit measure for hills, to worm it and weed it, to prune it and dress it as occasion shall require.

These Indians be very hospitable, insomuch that when the English have traveled forty, fifty, or threescore miles into the country, they have entertained them into their houses, quartered them by themselves in the best rooms, providing the best victuals they could, expressing their welcome in as good terms as could be expected from their slender breeding; showing more love than compliment, not grumbling for a fortnight's or three weeks' tarrying but rather caring to provide accommodation correspondent to their English custom. The doubtful traveler hath oftentimes been much beholding to them for their guidance through the unbeaten wilderness. Myself in this particular can do no less in the due acknowledgement of their love than speak their commendations, who with two more of my associates bending our course to New Plymmouth lost our way, being deluded by a misleading path which we still followed, being as we thought too broad for an Indian path (which seldom is broader than a cart's rut) but that the daily concourse of Indians from the Narragansetts who traded for shoes, wearing them homewards, had made this Indian tract like an English walk and had reared up great sticks against the trees and marked the rest with their hatchets in the English fashion, which begat in us a security of our wrong way to be right when indeed there was nothing less. The day being gloomy and our compasses at home, we traveled hard till night to less purpose than if we had sat still, not gaining an inch of our journey for a day's travel. But happily we arrived at an Indian wigwam where we were informed of our misprision and invited to a homely lodging, feasted with the haunch of a fat bear, and the ensuing morning the son of my naked host, for a piece of tobacco and a four penny whittle, took the clue of his traveling experience, conducting us through the strange labyrinth of unbeaten bushy ways in the woody wilderness twenty miles to our desired harbor.

A second demonstration of their love in this kind may appear in a passage of the same nature. An unexperienced woodman, ranging in the woods for deer, traveled so far beyond his knowledge till he could not tell how to get out of the wood for trees, but the more he sought to direct himself out, the more he ran himself in, from the home he most desired. The night came upon him, preventing his walking, and the extremity of cold seizing upon his right foot for want of warming motion, deprived him of the use thereof, so that he could not remove farther than his snowy bed, but had there ended his days had not six commiserating Indians who heard of his wandering found him out by diligent search, being almost dead with despair and cold. But after they had conquered his despair with the assurance of his habitation,[31] and expelled the cold by the infusion of strong waters which they brought for the same purpose, they framed a thing like a hand barrow and carried this self-helpless person on their bare shoulders twelve miles to his residence.

Many other wandering, benighted coasters have been kindly entertained into their habitations, where they have rested and reposed themselves more securely than if they had been in some blind obscure old England's inn, being the next day directed in their right way. Many lazy boys that have run away from their masters have been brought home by these ranging foresters, who are as well acquainted with the craggy mountains and the pleasant vales, the stately woods and swampy groves, the spacious ponds and swift-running rivers, and can distinguish

31. "Safe conduct to his" precedes "habitation" in the 1634 edition but not in the 1635 and 1639 editions.

them by their names as perfectly and find them as presently as the experienced citizen knows how to find out Cheapside Cross or London Stone.

Such is the wisdom and policy of these poor men that they will be sure to keep correspondence with our English magistrates, expressing their love in the execution of any service they command them (so far as lies in their power), as may appear in this one particular: A certain man having laid himself open to the king's laws, fearing attachment, conviction, and consequently execution, sequestered himself from the honest society of his neighbors, betaking himself unto the obscure thickets of the wilderness where he lived for a time undiscovered till the Indians, who leave no place unsearched for deer, found out his haunt, and having taken notice by diverse discourses concerning him how that it was the governor's desire to know where he was, they thought it part of their service to certify him where he kept his rendezvous, who thereupon desired if they could to direct men to him for his attachment. But he had shifted his dwelling and could not be found for the present, yet he was after seen by other Indians, but being double-pistoled and well-sworded, they feared to approach so near him as to grapple with him. Wherefore they let him alone till his own necessary business cast him upon them; for having occasion to cross a river, he came to the side thereof where was an Indian canoe in which the Indians were to cross the river themselves. He vauntingly commanded waftage, which they willingly granted but withal plotting how they might take him prisoner, which they thus effected: having placed him in the midship of their ticklish wherry, they launched forth into the deep, causing the capering canoe to cast out her cumbersome ballast into the liquid water, which swam like a stone. And now the water having danked his pistols and lost his Spanish prog[32] in the bottom, the Indians swam him out by the chin to the shore, where having dropped himself a little dry, he began to bluster out a storm of rebellious resistance till they becalmed his pelting chafe with their pelting of pebbles at him, afterward leading him as they list to the governor.

These people be of a kind and affable disposition, yet are they very wary with whom they strike hands in friendship. Nothing is more hateful to them than a churlish disposition, so likewise is dissimulation; he that speaks seldom and opportunely, being as good as his word, is the only man they love. The Spaniard they say is all one aramouse (viz., all

32. A spike or stiletto.

one as a dog); the Frenchman hath a good tongue but a false heart; the Englishman all one speak, all one heart, wherefore they more approve of them than of any nation. Garrulity is much condemned of them, for they utter not many words, speak seldom, and then with such gravity as is pleasing to the ear. Such as understand them not desire yet to hear their emphatical expressions and lively action.

Such is the mild temper of their spirits that they cannot endure objurgations or scoldings. An Indian sagamore once hearing an English woman scold with her husband, her quick utterance exceeding his apprehension, her active lungs thundering in his ears, expelled him [from] the house; from whence he went to the next neighbor where he related the unseemliness of her behavior. Her language being strange to him, he expressed it as strangely, telling them how she cried *"Nannana, Nannana, Nannana, Nan,"* saying he was a great fool to give her the audience and no correction for usurping his charter and abusing him by her tongue.

I have been amongst diverse of them, yet did I never see any falling out amongst them, not so much as cross words or reviling speeches which might provoke to blows. And whereas it is the custom of many people in their games, if they see the dice run cross or their cards not answer their expectations,what cursing and swearing, what imprecations and railings, fightings and stabbings oftentimes proceed from their testy spleen. How do their blustering passions make the place troublesome to themselves and others? But I have known when four of these milder spirits have sit down, staking their treasures, where they have played four and twenty hours, neither eating, drinking, or sleeping in the interim; nay which is most to be wondered at, not quarreling, but as they came thither in peace so they depart in peace. When he that had lost all his wampompeag, his house, his kettle, his beaver, his hatchet, his knife, yea all his little all, having nothing left but his naked self, was as merry as they that won it. So in sports of activity: at football (though they play never so fiercely to outward appearance, yet angrier-boiling blood never streams in their cooler veins) if any man be thrown, he laughs out his foil. There is no seeking of revenge, no quarreling, no bloody noses, scratched faces, black eyes, broken shins, no bruised members or crushed ribs, the lamentable effects of rage. But the goal being won, the goods on the one side lost, friends they were at the football and friends they must meet at the kettle.

I never heard yet of that Indian that was his neighbor's homicide or vexation by his malipart,[33] saucy, or uncivil tongue. Laughter in them is not common, seldom exceeding a smile, never breaking out into such a loud laughter as do many of our English. Of all things they love not to be laughed at upon any occasion. If a man be in trade with them and the bargain be almost struck, if they perceive you laugh they will scarce proceed, supposing you laugh because you have cheated them. The crocodile's tears may sooner deceive them than the hyena's smiles. Although they be not much addicted to laughter, yet are they not of a dumpish, sad nature, but rather naturally cheerful. As I never saw a giggling Democrite,[34] so I never saw a tear-dropping Heraclite,[35] no disaster being so prevalent as to open the floodgate of their eyes saving the death of friends, for whom they lament most exceedingly.

CHAP. 8

Of Their Hardiness.

For their hardiness it may procure admiration, no ordinary pains making them so much as alter their countenance. Beat them, whip them, pinch them, punch them, if they resolve not to winch for it, they will not. Whether it be their benumbed insensibleness of smart, or their hardy resolutions, I cannot tell. It might be [that] a Perillus his bull[36] or the disjointing rack might force a roar from them, but a Turkish drubbing would not much molest them. And although they be naturally much afraid of death, yet the unexpected approach of a mortal wound by a bullet, arrow, or sword strikes no more terror, causes no more exclamation, no more complaint or winching than if it had been a shot into the body of a tree.

Such wounds as would be sudden death to an Englishman would be nothing to them: some of them having been shot in at the mouth and out under the ear, some shot in the breast, some run through the flanks with darts, and other many desperate wounds which either by their rare

33. Variant form of "malapert"—bold, impudent.
34. Democritus, the "laughing philosopher" of fifth century B.C. Greece.
35. Heraclitus, the "weeping philosopher" of fifth century B.C. Greece.
36. The hollow bronze bull of the tyrant Phalaris, in which criminals were roasted to death. Built by Perillus (ca. 550 B.C.) who became its first victim.

skill in the use of vegetatives or diabolical charms they cure in short time.[37]

Although their hardiness bear them out in such things wherein they are sure death will not ensue, yet can it not dispel the fear of death; the very name and thoughts of it is so hideous to them, or anything that presents it or threatens it so terrible, insomuch that a hundred of them will run from two or three guns though they know they can but dispatch two or three at a discharge. Yet every man, fearing it may be his lot to meet with his last, will not come near that in good earnest which he dare play withal in jest. To make this good by a passage of experience: three men having occasion of trade amongst the western Indians went up with some such commodities as they thought most fit for trade. To secure their person they took a carbine, two pistols, and a sword, which in outward show was not great resistance to a hundred well-skilled bowmen. The Indians hearing their guns making a thundering noise desired to finger one of them and see it discharged into a tree, wondering much at the percussion of the bullet. But they abiding two or three days, the guns were forgotten and they began to look at the odds (being a hundred to three), whereupon they were animated to work treason against the lives of these men and to take away their goods from them by force. But one of the English, understanding their language, smelt out their treachery, and being more fully informed of their intent by the Indian women, who had more pity, he steps to their king and hailing him by the long hair from the rest of his council commanded him either to go before him and guide him home or else he would there kill him. The sagamore seeing him so rough had not the courage to resist him, but went with him two miles. But being exasperated by his men who followed him along to resist and go no further, in the end he would not, neither for the fair promises nor fierce threatenings, so that they were constrained there to kill him, which struck such an amazement and daunting into the rest of that naked crew, with the sight of the guns, that though they might easily have killed them, yet had they not the power to shoot an arrow, but followed them, yelling and howling for the death of their king, forty miles. His goods being left among them, he sent word by other Indians that unless they sent him his goods again, which he there

37. On Indian remedies for wounds and diseases see Williams, *Key into the Language,* chap. 31; and Virgil J. Vogel, *American Indian Medicine* (Norman, Okla., 1970).

left, he would serve them as he served their king, whereupon they returned him his commodities with entreaty of peace and promises of fairer trade if he came again.

If these heartless Indians were so cowed with so slender an onset on their own dunghill, when there were scarce six families of ours in the country, what need we now fear them, being grown into thousands and having knowledge of martial discipline? In the night they need not to be feared for they will not budge from their own dwellings for fear of their Abamacho (the Devil) whom they much fear, especially in evil enterprises. They will rather lie by an English fire than go a quarter of a mile in the dark to their own dwellings. But they are well freed from this scarecrow since the coming of the English and less care for his delusions. And whereas it hath been reported that there are such horrible apparitions, fearful roarings, thundering and lightning raised by the Devil to discourage the English in their settling, I for mine own part never saw or heard of any of these things in the country. Nor have I heard of any Indians that have lately been put in fear, saving two or three, and they worse scared than hurt, who seeing a blackamore in the top of a tree, looking out for his way which he had lost, surmised he was Abamacho or the Devil (deeming all devils that are blacker than themselves) and being near to the plantation they posted to the English and entreated their aide to conjure this devil to his own place, who finding him to be a poor wandering blackamore, conducted him to his master.[38]

CHAP. 9

Of Their Wondering at the First View of
Any Strange Invention.

These Indians being strangers to arts and sciences, and being unacquainted with the inventions that are common to a civilized people, are ravished with admiration at the first view of any such sight. They took the first ship they saw for a walking island, the mast to be a tree, the sail white clouds, and the discharging of ordnance for lightning and thunder,

38. For another seventeenth-century view of the Indians' "Diabolical Art" see John Josselyn, *An Account of Two Voyages to New England* (London, 1675; repr. Massachusetts Historical Society, *Collections*, 3rd ser. 3 [1833]), 300f.

which did much trouble them, but this thunder being over and this moving-island steadied with an anchor, they manned out their canoes to go and pick strawberries there. But being saluted by the way with a broadside, they cried out, "What much hoggery, so big walk, and so big speak, and by and by kill"; which caused them to turn back, not daring to approach till they were sent for.[39]

They do much extol and wonder at the English for their strange inventions, especially for a windmill which in their esteem was little less than the world's wonder, for the strangeness of his whisking motion and the sharp teeth biting the corn (as they term it) into such small pieces, they were loath at the first to come near to his long arms, or to abide in so tottering a tabernacle, though now they dare go anywhere so far as they have an English guide. The first plowman was counted little better than a juggler: the Indians, seeing the plow tear up more ground in a day than their clamshells could scrape up in a month, desired to see the workmanship of it, and viewing well the coulter and share, perceiving it to be iron, told the plowman he was almost Abamacho, almost as cunning as the Devil. But the fresh supplies of new and strange objects hath lessened their admiration and quickened their inventions and desire of practising such things as they see, wherein they express no small ingenuity and dexterity of wit, being neither furthered by art [n]or long experience.

It is thought they would soon learn any mechanical trades, having quick wits, understanding apprehensions, strong memories, with nimble inventions, and a quick hand in using of the ax or hatchet or such like tools. Much good might they receive from the English, and much might they benefit themselves, if they were not strong fettered in the chains of idleness; so as that they had rather starve than work, following no employments saving such as are sweetened with more pleasures and profit than pains or care, and this is indeed one of the greatest accusations that can be laid against them which lies but upon the men (the women being very industrious). But it may be hoped that good example and good instructions may bring them to a more industrious and provident course of life, for already, as they have learned much subtlety and cunning by bargaining with the English, so have they a little degenerated

39. For comments on the Indians' reaction to the arrival of Europeans see Edward Johnson, *Johnson's Wonder-Working Providence, 1628-1651* (ed. J. Franklin Jameson, New York, 1910), pp. 39-40, 43.

from some of their lazy customs and show themselves more industrious.

In a word, to set them out in their best colors, they be wise in their carriage, subtle in their dealings, true in their promise, honest in defraying of their debts, though poverty constrain them to be something long before. Some having died in the English debt had left beaver by order of will for their satisfaction. They be constant in friendship, merrily conceited in discourse, not luxuriously abounding in youth nor dotingly forward in old age, many of them being much civilized since the English colonies were planted, though but little edified in religion. They frequent often the English churches where they will sit soberly, though they understand not such hidden mysteries. They do easily believe some of the history of the Bible, as the creation of the world, the making of man, with his fall. But come to tell them of a Saviour, with all the passages of the Gospel, and it exceeds so far their Indian belief that they will cry out *"Pocatnie"* (*id est*, is it possible?). Yet such is their conviction of the right way that when some English have come to their houses, victuals being offered them, forgetting to crave God's blessing upon the creatures received, they have been reproved by these which formerly never knew what calling upon God meant. Thus far for their natural disposition and qualities.

CHAP. 10

*Of Their Kings' Government
and Subjects' Obedience.*

Now for the matter of government amongst them. It is the custom for their kings to inherit, the son always taking the kingdom after his father's death. If there be no son, then the queen rules; if no queen, the next to the blood-royal.[40] Who comes in otherwise is but counted an usurping intruder, and if his fair carriage bear him not out the better, they will soon unscepter him.

The kings have not many laws[41] to command by, nor have they any

40. Many Indians, perhaps all of the New England tribes, traced descent through the maternal side of the family.
41. The 1634 edition reads "no laws," which is replaced by "not many laws" in the 1635 and 1639 editions.

annual revenues; yet commonly are they so either feared or beloved that half their subjects' estate is at their service and their persons at his command, by which command he is better known than by anything else. For though he hath no kingly robes to make him glorious in the view of his subjects, nor daily guards to secure his person, or court-like attendance, nor sumptuous palaces, yet do they yield all submissive subjection to him, accounting him their sovereign, going at his command and coming at his beck, not so much as expostulating the cause though it be in matters thwarting their wills, he being accounted a disloyal subject that will not effect what his prince commands.[42]

Whosoever is known to plot treason or to lay violent hands on his lawful king is presently executed. Once a year he takes his progress, accompanied with a dozen of his best subjects, to view his country, to recreate himself, and establish good order. When he enters into any of their houses, without any more compliment he is desired to sit down on the ground (for they use neither stools nor cushions), and after a little respite all that be present come in and sit down by him, one of his seniors pronouncing an oration gratulatory to his majesty for his love and the many good things they enjoy under his peaceful government.

A king of large dominions hath his viceroys, or inferior kings, under him to agitate his state affairs and keep his subjects in good decorum. Other officers there be, but how to distinguish them by name is something difficult. For their laws, as their evil courses come short of many other nations', so they have not so many laws, though they be not without some which they inflict upon notorious malefactors, as traitors to their prince, inhumane murtherers, and (some say) for adultery, but I cannot warrant it for a truth. For theft, as they have nothing to steal worth the life of a man, therefore they have no law to execute for trivials, a subject being precious in the eye of his prince where men are so scarce. A malefactor having deserved death, being apprehended is brought before the king and some other of the wisest men, where they inquire out the original of a thing. After proceeding by aggravation of

42. On government among the New England tribes see Williams, *Key into the Language,* chap. 21; and Gookin, *Historical Collections,* p. 20. For a comparison with the Indians of Virginia see Edward Arber and A.G. Bradley, eds., *Travels and Works of Captain John Smith* (2 vols., Edinburgh, 1910), 1, 79–82. For a modern perspective see Anthony F.C. Wallace, "Political Organization and Land Tenure among the Northeastern Indians, 1600–1830," *Southwestern Journal of Anthropology,* 13 (1957), 301–321.

circumstances, he is found guilty, and being cast by the jury of their strict inquisition, he is condemned and executed on this manner: the executioner comes in, who blindfolds the party, sets him in the public view, and brains him with a tomahawk or club; which done, his friends bury him. Other means to restrain abuses they have none, saving admonition or reproof; no whippings, no prisons, stocks, bilboes, or the like.

CHAP. 11

Of Their Marriages.

Now to speak something of their marriages. The kings or great powwows, alias conjurers, may have two or three wives but seldom use it, men of ordinary rank having but one; which disproves the report that they had eight or ten wives apiece. When a man hath a desire to marry, he first gets the good will of the maid or widow; after, the consent of her friends for her part. And for himself, if he be at his own disposing, if the king will, the match is made, her dowry of wampompeag paid, the king joins their hands with their hearts, never to part till death unless she prove a whore, for which they may (and some have) put away their wives, as may appear by a story.

There was one Abamoch married a wife, whom a long time he entirely loved above her deservings, for that she often in his absence entertained strangers, of which he was oftentimes informed by his neighbors. But he harboring no spark of jealousy, believed not their false informations (as he deemed them) being in a manner angry they should slander his wife, of whose constancy he was so strongly conceited. A long time did her whorish glozing[43] and Siren-like tongue, with her subtle carriage, establish her in her husband's favor till fresh complaints caused him to cast about how to find out the truth and to prove his friends liars and his wife honest, or her a whore and his friends true. Whereupon he pretended a long journey to visit his friends, providing all accoutrements for a fortnight's journey, telling his wife it would be so long before she could expect his return, who outwardly sorrowed for his departure but inwardly rejoiced that she should enjoy the society of her old leman, whom she sent for with expedition, not suspecting her husband's plot, who lay

43. I.e., coaxing.

not many miles off in the woods; who, after their dishonest revelings, when they were in their midnight sleep, approaches the wigwam, enters the door, which was neither barred nor locked, makes a light to discover what he little suspected. But finding his friends' words to be true, he takes a good bastinado in his hand, brought for the same purpose, dragging him by the hair from his usurped bed, so lamentably beating him that his battered bones and bruised flesh made him a fitter subject for some skillful surgeon than the lovely object of a lustful strumpet. Which done, he put away his wife, exposing her to the courtesy of strangers for her maintenance, that so courtesan-like had entertained a stranger into her bosom.[44]

CHAP. 12

Of Their Worship, Invocations, and Conjurations.

Now of their worships. As it is natural to all mortals to worship something, so do these people, but exactly to describe to whom their worship is chiefly bent is very difficult. They acknowledge especially two: Ketan who is their good god, to whom they sacrifice (as the ancient heathen did to Ceres) after their garners be full with a good crop; upon this god likewise they invoke for fair weather, for rain in time of drought, and for the recovery of their sick.

But if they do not hear them, then they verify the old verse, *flectere si nequeo superos, acharonta movebo,*[45] their powwows betaking themselves to their exorcisms and necromantic charms by which they bring to pass strange things, if we may believe the Indians who report of one Passaconaway that he can make the water burn, the rocks move, the

---

44. On courtship and marriage among the Indians of New England see Williams, *Key into the Language,* chap. 23; and Gookin, *Historical Collections,* p. 13. For marriage customs outside New England see Adrien Van der Donck, *A Description of the New Netherland,* ed. Thomas F. O'Donnell (Syracuse, 1968), pp. 82–84; John Lawson, *A New Voyage to Carolina* (Richmond, Va., 1937), pp. 196–200; and John Heckewelder, *History, Manners, and Customs of the Indian Nations Who Once Inhabited Pennsylvania and the Neighboring States,* ed. William C. Reichel (Historical Society of Pennsylvania, *Memoirs* 13 [Philadelphia, 1871; rev. ed., 1876; repr. New York, 1971]), pp. 154–162.

45. Transl.: "If I cannot sway the gods above, I'll stir up Hell." From Vergil's *Aeneid.*

trees dance, metamorphise himself into a flaming man. But it may be objected, this is but *deceptio visus*.[46] He will therefore do more, for in winter, when there is no green leaves to be got, he will burn an old one to ashes, and putting those into the water produce a new green leaf which you shall not only see but substantially handle and carry away, and make of a dead snake's skin a living snake, both to be seen, felt, and heard. This I write but on the report of the Indians, who constantly affirm stranger things.

But to make manifest that by God's permission, through the Devil's help, their charms are of force to produce effects of wonderment, an honest gentleman related a story to me, being an eyewitness of the same: a powwow having a patient with the stump of some small tree run through his foot, being past the cure of his ordinary surgery, betook himself to his charms, and being willing to show his miracle before the English stranger, he wrapped a piece of cloth about the foot of the lame man [and] upon that wrapping a beaver skin through which he—laying his mouth to the beaver skin—by his sucking charms he brought out the stump which he spat into a tray of water, returning the foot as whole as its fellow in a short time.

The manner of their action in their conjuration is thus: the parties that are sick or lame being brought before them, the powwow sitting down, the rest of the Indians giving attentive audience to his imprecations and invocations, and after the violent expression of many a hideous bellowing and groaning, he makes a stop, and then all the auditors with one voice utter a short canto. Which done, the powwow still proceeds in his invocations, sometimes roaring like a bear, other times groaning like a dying horse, foaming at the mouth like a chased boar, smiting on his naked breast and thighs with such violence as if he were mad. Thus will he continue sometimes half a day, spending his lungs, sweating out his fat, and tormenting his body in this diabolical worship. Sometimes the Devil for requital of their worship recovers the party, to nuzzle them up in their devilish religion. In former time he was wont to carry away their wives and children, because he would drive them to these matins[47] to fetch them again to confirm their belief of this, his much desired authority over them. But since the English frequented those parts, they daily fall from his colors, relinquishing their former

46. Transl.: "a delusion of sight."
47. I.e., religious services. Wood here implies devil worship.

fopperies, and acknowledge our God to be supreme. They acknowledge the power of the Englishman's God, as they call him, because they could never yet have power by their conjurations to damnify the English either in body or goods; and besides, they say he is a good God that sends them so many good things, so much good corn, so many cattle, temperate rains, fair seasons, which they likewise are the better for since the arrival of the English, the times and seasons being much altered in seven or eight years, freer from lightning and thunder, long droughts, sudden and tempestuous dashes of rain, and lamentable cold winters.[48]

CHAP. 13

Of Their Wars.

Of their wars: their old soldiers being swept away by the plague which was very rife amongst them about fourteen years ago,[49] and resting themselves secure under the English protection, they do not now practice anything in martial feats worth observation, saving that they make themselves forts to fly into if the enemies should unexpectedly assail them. These forts some be forty or fifty foot square, erected of young timber trees ten or twelve foot high, rammed into the ground, with undermining within, the earth being cast up for their shelter against the dischargements of their enemies, having loopholes to send out their winged messengers, which often deliver their sharp and bloody embassies in the tawny sides of their naked assailants, who wanting buttingrams and battering ordnances to command at distance, lose their lives by their too near approachments.[50]

48. For other accounts of Indian religion see Morton, *New English Canaan,* pp. 27f.; Williams, *Key into the Language,* chap. 21; Gookin, *Historical Collections,* p. 20; and Josselyn, *Two Voyages,* pp. 300f.
49. The Europeans who came to New England settled in an area recently devastated by the plague. On the impact of European diseases see Vaughan, *New England Frontier,* pp. 21f.; John Duffy, "Smallpox and the Indians in the American Colonies," *Bulletin of the History of Medicine,* 25 (1951), 324-341; Sherburne F. Cook, "The Significance of Disease in the Extinction of the New England Indians," *Human Biology,* 44 (1973), 485-508; and Jennings, *Invasion of America,* pp. 15-31.
50. Northeastern tribes usually surrounded their villages with palisades for defense against other tribes and later against Europeans.

These [people] use no other weapons in war than bows and arrows, saving that their captains have long spears on which, if they return conquerors, they carry the heads of their chief enemies that they slay in the wars, it being the custom to cut off their heads, hands, and feet to bear home to their wives and children as true tokens of their renowned victory.[51] When they go to their wars, it is their custom to paint their faces with diversity of colors, some being all black as jet, some red, some half red and half black, some black and white, others spotted with diverse kinds of colors, being all disguised to their enemies to make them more terrible to their foes, putting on likewise their rich jewels, pendants, and wampompeag, to put them in mind they fight not only for their children, wives, and lives, but likewise for their goods, lands, and liberties. Being thus armed with this warlike paint, the antic warriors make towards their enemies in a disordered manner, without any soldier-like marching or warlike postures, being deaf to any word of command, ignorant of falling off or falling on, of doubling ranks or files, but let fly their winged shaftments without either fear or wit. Their artillery being spent, he that hath no arms to fight, finds legs to run away.

CHAP. 14

Their Games and Sports of Activity.

But to leave their wars, and to speak of their games in which they are more delighted and better experienced, spending half their days in gaming and lazing: they have two sorts of games, one called puim, the other hubbub, not much unlike cards and dice, being no other than lottery.[52]

Puim is fifty or sixty small bents[53] of a foot long, which they divide to the number of their gamesters, shuffling them first between the palms

---

51. Many early English chroniclers commented on the Indian practice of scalping. See, for example, Williams, *Key into the Language*, p. 131; William Hubbard, *The History of the Indian Wars in New England* (2 vols., Roxbury, Mass., 1865; repr. New York, 1969), 2, 206; Gookin, *Historical Collections*, p. 22; and Charles Orr, ed., *History of the Pequot War* (Cleveland, 1897), p. 138. For a modern assessment see Axtell, "Scholastic Philosophy," 344–346.
52. On Indian gambling see Williams, *Key into the Language*, chap. 28; Gookin, *Historical Collections*, p. 19; and James Adair, *History of the American Indians,* ed. Samuel Cole Williams (Johnson City, Tenn., 1930), pp. 428–431.
53. I.e., rushes. See Williams, *Key into the Language*, chap. 28.

of their hands; he that hath more than his fellow is so much the for-warder in his game. Many other strange whimseys be in this game, which would be too long to commit to paper. He that is a noted gamester hath a great hole in his ear wherein he carries his puims in defiance of his antagonists.

Hubbub is five small bones in a small, smooth tray; the bones be like a die but something flatter, black on the one side and white on the other, which they place on the ground, against which violently thumping the platter, the bones mount, changing colors with the windy whisking of their hands to and fro; which action in that sport they much use, smiting themselves on the breast and thighs, crying out "*hub, hub, hub, hub.*" They may be heard play[ing] at this game a quarter of a mile off. The bones being all black or white make a double game; if three be of a color and two of another, then they afford but a single game; four of a color and one differing is nothing. So long as a man wins he keeps the tray, but if he lose, the next man takes it. They are so bewitched with these two games that they will lose sometimes all they have—beaver, moose skins, kettles, wampompeag, mowhacheis, hatchets, knives—all is confiscate by these two games.

For their sports of activity they have commonly but three or four, as football, shooting, running, and swimming. When they play country against country there are rich goals, all behung with wampompeag, mowhacheis, beaver skins, and black otter skins. It would exceed the belief of many to relate the worth of one goal, wherefore it shall be nameless. Their goals be a mile long, placed on the sands, which are as even as a board. Their ball is no bigger than a handball, which sometimes they mount in the air with their naked feet; sometimes it is swayed by the multitude; sometimes also it is two days before they get a goal. Then they mark the ground they win and begin there the next day.

Before they come to this sport, they paint themselves, even as when they go to war, in policy to prevent future mischief because no man should know him that moved his patience or accidentally hurt his person, taking away the occasion of studying revenge. Before they begin their arms be disordered and hung upon some neighboring tree, after which they make a long scroll on the sand over which they shake loving hands, and with laughing hearts scuffle for victory. While the men play, the boys pipe and the women dance and sing trophies of their husbands' conquests. All being done, a feast summons their departure. It is most delight to see them play in smaller companies, when men may view their swift footmanship, their curious tossings of their ball, their flouncing into the water, their lubberlike wrestling, having no cunning at all in that kind, one English being able to beat ten Indians at football.

For their shooting they be most desperate marksmen for a point blank object, and if it may be possible, *cornicum oculos configere,*[54] they will do it. Such is their celerity and dexterity in artillery that they can smite the swift-running hind and nimble-winked pigeon without a standing pause or left-eyed blinking. They draw their arrows between the fore-fingers and the thumb. Their bows be quick but not very strong, not killing above six or seven score. These men shoot at one another, but with swift conveyance shun the arrow. This they do to make them expert against time of war. It hath been often admired how they can find their arrows; be the weeds as high as themselves, yet they take such perfect notice of the flight and fall that they seldom lose any. They are trained up to their bows even from their childhood; little boys with bows made of little sticks and arrows of great bents will smite down a piece of tobacco pipe every shoot a good way off. As these Indians be good marksmen, so are they well experienced where the very life of every creature lieth, and know where to smite him to make him die presently.

For their swimming, it is almost natural, but much perfected by continual practise. Their swimming is not after our English fashion of spread arms and legs, which they hold too tiresome, but like dogs their arms before them cutting through the liquids with their right shoulder. In this manner they swim very swift and far, either in rough or smooth waters, sometimes for their ease lying as still as a log. Sometimes they will play the dive-doppers and come up in unexpected places. Their children likewise be taught to swim when they are very young.

For their running, it is with much celerity and continuance, yet I suppose there be many Englishmen who, being as lightly clad as they are, would outrun them for a spurt, though not able to continue it for a day or days, being they be very strong-winded and rightly clad for a race.

---

54. Transl.: "to feign crow's eyes." Wood probably intended the proverb, "to deceive the most wary," which was based on an ancient belief in the mystic powers of crows.

CHAP. 15

Of Their Huntings.

For their hunting, it is to be noted that they have no swift-foot grey-hounds to let slip at the sight of the deer, no deep-mouthed hounds or scenting beagles to find out their desired prey; themselves are all this, who in that time of the year when the deer come down, having certain hunting houses in such places where they know the deer usually doth frequent, in which they keep their rendezvous, their snares, and all their accoutrements for that employment. When they get sight of a deer, moose, or bear, they study how to get the wind of him, and approaching within shot, stab their mark quite through, if the bones hinder not.[55]

The chief thing they hunt after is deer, mooses, and bears; it grieves them more to see an Englishman take one deer than a thousand acres of land. They hunt likewise after wolves and wildcats, raccoons, otters, beavers, musquashes, trading both their skins and flesh to the English.

Besides their artillery, they have other devices to kill their game, as sometimes hedges a mile or two miles long, being a mile wide at one end and made narrower and narrower by degrees, leaving only a gap of six foot long over against which, in the daytime, they lie lurking to shoot the deer which come through that narrow gut. So many as come within the circumference of that hedge seldom return back to leap over, unless they be forced by the chasing of some ravenous wolf or sight of some accidental passenger. In the night, at the gut of this hedge they set deer traps, which are springs made of young trees and smooth-wrought cords, so strong as it will toss a horse if he be caught in it.

An English mare being strayed from her owner and grown wild by her long sojourning in the woods, ranging up and down with the wild crew, stumbled into one of these traps which stopped her speed, hanging her like Mahomet's tomb betwixt earth and heaven. The morning being come, the Indians went to look what good success their venison traps had brought them, but seeing such a long-scutted[56] deer prance in their merrytotter,[57] they bade her good morrow, crying out, "What cheer, what cheer Englishman's squaw horse"—having no better epithet than

---

55. On Indian hunting see Williams, *Key into the Language,* chap. 27; and John Lawson, *A New Voyage to Carolina* (Richmond, Va., 1937), pp. 219–223.
56. I.e., long tailed.
57. I.e., a swing or seesaw.

to call her a woman's horse. But being loath to kill her, and as fearful to approach near the friscadoes[58] of her iron heels, they posted to the English to tell them how the case stood, or hung, with their squaw horse, who unhorsed their mare and brought her to her former tameness, which since hath brought many a good foal and performed much good service.

In these traps deers, mooses, bears, wolves, cats, and foxes are often caught.[59] For their beavers and otters, they have other kind of traps, so ponderous as is unsupportable for such creatures, the massy burthen whereof either takes them prisoners or expels their breath from their squeezed bodies. These kind of creatures would gnaw the other kind of traps asunder with their sharp teeth. These beasts are too cunning for the English, who seldom or never catch any of them; therefore we leave them to those skillful hunters whose time is not so precious, whose experience-bought skill hath made them practical and useful in that particular.

CHAP. 16

Of Their Fishings.

Of their fishing: in this trade they be very expert, being experienced in the knowledge of all baits, fitting sundry baits for several fishes and diverse seasons; being not ignorant likewise of the removal of fishes, knowing when to fish rivers and when at rocks, when in bays, and when at seas. Since the English came they be furnished with English hooks and lines; before they made them of their own hemp more curiously wrought of stronger materials than ours, hooked with bone hooks, but laziness drives them to buy more than profit or commendations wins them to make of their own. They make likewise very strong sturgeon nets with which they catch sturgeons of twelve, fourteen, and sixteen, some eighteen foot long in the daytime. In the nighttime they betake them to their birchen canoes, in which they carry a forty-fathom line with a sharp, bearded dart fastened at the end thereof. Then lighting a

58. I.e., capering or brisk dancing.
59. Unwary Englishmen occasionally got caught too. See Dwight B. Heath, ed., *A Journal of the Pilgrims at Plymouth: Mourt's Relation* (New York, 1963), p. 23, for William Bradford's encounter with a deer trap.

blazing torch made of birchen rinds, they weave it to and again by their canoe side, which the sturgeon, much delighted with, comes to them tumbling and playing, turning up his white belly, into which they thrust their lance, his back being impenetrable. Which done, they hail to the shore their struggling prize. They have often recourse unto the rocks whereupon the sea beats, in warm weather, to look out for sleepy seals, whose oil they much esteem, using it for diverse things. In summer they seldom fish anywhere but in salt; in winter in the fresh water and ponds. In frosty weather they cut round holes in the ice, about which they will sit like so many apes, on their naked breeches upon the congealed ice, catching of pikes, perches, breams, and other sorts of fresh water fish.[60]

CHAP. 17

Of Their Arts and Manufactures.

Of their several arts and employments, as first in dressing of all manner of skins, which they do by scraping and rubbing, afterwards painting them with antic embroiderings in unchangeable colors. Sometimes they take off the hair, especially if it be not killed in season. Their bows they make of a handsome shape, strung commonly with the sinews of mooses; their arrows are made of young eldern, feathered with feathers of eagles' wings and tails, headed with brass in shape of a heart or triangle, fastened in a slender piece of wood six or eight inches long which is framed to put loose in the pithy eldern that is bound fast for riving. Their arrows be made in this manner because the arrow might shake from his head and be left behind for their finding, and the pile only remain to gall the wounded beast.

Their cordage is so even, soft, and smooth that it looks more like silk than hemp. Their sturgeon nets be not deep, nor above thirty or forty foot long, which in ebbing low waters they stake fast to the ground where they are sure the sturgeon will come, never looking more at it till the next low water. Their canoes be made either of pine trees, which be-

60. For other accounts of Indian fishing techniqes see Williams, *Key into the Language,* chap. 19; Josselyn, *Two Voyages to New England,* pp. 305f.; and Frank G. Speck and Ralph W. Dexter, "Utilization of Marine Life by the Wampanoag Indians of Massachusetts," *Journal of the Washington Academy of Sciences,* 48 (1948), 257–265.

fore they were acquainted with English tools they burned hollow, scraping them smooth with clam shells and oyster shells, cutting their outsides with stone hatchets. These boats be not above a foot and a half or two feet wide and twenty foot long. Their other canoes be made of thin birch rinds, close ribbed on the inside with broad, thin hoops like the hoops of a tub. These are made very light. A man may carry one of them a mile, being made purposely to carry from river to river and bay to bay, to shorten land passages. In these cockling fly-boats, wherein an Englishman can scarce sit without a fearful tottering, they will venture to sea when an English shallop dare not bear a knot of sail, scudding over the overgrown waves as fast as a wind-driven ship, being driven by their paddles, being much like battledores. If a cross wave (as is seldom) turn her keel upside down, they by swimming free her and scramble into her again.

CHAP. 18

Of Their Language.

Of their language, which is only peculiar to themselves, not inclining to any of the refined tongues: some have thought they might be of the dispersed Jews because some of their words be near unto the Hebrew, but by the same rule they may conclude them to be of some of the gleanings of all nations because they have words which sound after the Greek, Latin, French, and other tongues. Their language is hard to learn, few of the English being able to speak any of it, or capable of the right pronunciation, which is the chief grace of their tongue. They pronounce much after the dipthongs, excluding L and R, which in our English tongue they pronounce with as much difficulty as most of the Dutch do T and H, calling a lobster a *nobstann.*[61]

61. The most comprehensive discussion of the Algonquian tongue by a contemporary of Wood's is Williams, *Key into the Language,* which is both a study of language and an ironic comparison of Indian and English civilizations. For glossaries from other Algonquian regions see Arber and Bradley, *Travels and Works of Captain John Smith,* 1, 44–46; and Heckewelder, *History, Manners, and Customs,* parts 2 and 3. See also James C. Pilling, *Bibliography of the Algonquian Languages* (Washington, D. C., 1891).

Every country do something differ in their speech, even as our northern people do from the southern, and western from them; especially the
Tarrenteens, whose tongues run so much upon R that they wharle[62]
much in pronunciation. When any ships come near the shore, they de-
mand whether they be King Charles his Tories, with such a rumbling
sound as if one were beating an unbraced drum. In serious discourse our
southern Indians use seldom any short colloquiums but speak their
minds at large without any interjected interruptions from any, the rest
giving diligent audience to his utterance. Which done, some or other re-
turns him as long an answer. They love not to speak *multa sed mul-
tum*;[63] seldom are their words and their deeds strangers. According to
the matter in discourse, so are their acting gestures in their expressions.

One of the English preachers, in a special good intent of doing good
to their souls, hath spent much time in attaining to their language,
wherein he is so good a proficient that he can speak to their understanding and they to his, much loving and respecting him for his love and
counsel. It is hoped that he may be an instrument of good amongst
them.[64] They love any man that can utter his mind in their words, yet
are they not a little proud that they can speak the English tongue, using
it as much as their own when they meet with such as can understand it,
puzzling stranger Indians, which sometimes visit them from more remote
places, with an unheard language.

CHAP. 19

Of Their Deaths, Burials, and Mourning.

Although the Indians be of lusty and healthful bodies, not experimentally knowing the catalogue of those health-wasting diseases which are incident to other countries, as fevers, pleurisies, callentures, agues, ob-

---

62. I.e., pronounce with a guttural sound.
63. Transl.: "many but much," by which Wood apparently meant "they say much
in few words."
64. Presumably John Eliot of Roxbury, the principal missionary and linguist in
early New England. On Eliot and other Puritan missionaries see Samuel Eliot Morison, *Builders of the Bay Colony* (Boston, 1930), ch. 10; Vaughan, *New England
Frontier*, chs. 9–11; William Kellaway, *The New England Company, 1649-1776*
(New York, 1962); and Ola Elizabeth Winslow, *John Eliot, "Apostle to the Indi-*

structions, consumptions, subfumigations,[65] convulsions, apoplexies, dropsies, gouts, stones, toothaches, pox, measles, or the like, but spin out the thread of their days to a fair length, numbering threescore, fourscore, some a hundred years, before the world's universal summoner cite them to the craving grave.

But the date of their life expired, and death's arrestment seizing upon them, all hope of recovery being past, then to behold and hear their throbbing sobs and deep-fetched sighs, their grief-wrung hands and tear-bedewed cheeks, their doleful cries, would draw tears from adamantine eyes that be but spectators of their mournful obsequies. The glut of their grief being past, they commit the corpses of their deceased friends to the ground, over whose grave is for a long time spent many a briny tear, deep groan, and Irish-like howlings, continuing annual mournings with a black, stiff paint on their faces. These are the mourners without hope, yet do they hold the immortality of the never-dying soul that it shall pass to the southwest Elysium, concerning which their Indian faith jumps much with the Turkish Alcoran, holding it to be a kind of paradise wherein they shall everlastingly abide, solacing themselves in odoriferous gardens, fruitful corn fields, green meadows, bathing their tawny hides in the cool streams of pleasant rivers, and shelter themselves from heat and cold in the sumptuous palaces framed by the skill of nature's curious contrivement; concluding that neither care nor pain shall molest them but that nature's bounty will administer all things with a voluntary contribution from the overflowing storehouse of their Elysian Hospital, at the portal whereof, they say, lies a great dog whose churlish snarlings deny a *pax intrantibus*[66] to unworthy intruders. Wherefore it is their custom to bury with them their bows and arrows and good store of their wampompeag and mowhacheis; the one to affright that affronting Cerberus,[67] the other to purchase more immense prerogatives in

---

ans" (Boston, 1968). For recent interpretations that are highly critical of Puritan motives see Neal Salisbury, "Red Puritans: The 'Praying Indians' of Massachusetts Bay and John Eliot," *William and Mary Quarterly,* 3rd ser. 31 (1974), 27-54; and Jennings, *The Invasion of America.*
65. Obsolete form of "suffumigation." Wood's meaning is not clear because subfumigation (fumigation from below) was a therapeutic treatment rather than a disease or ailment.
66. Transl.: "Peace to those entering."
67. In Greek and Roman mythology, Cerberus was the watchdog who guarded the entrance to Hades.

their paradise. For their enemies and loose livers, whom they account unworthy of this imaginary happiness, they say that they pass to the infernal dwellings of Abamacho, to be tortured according to the fictions of the ancient heathen.[68]

CHAP. 20

Of Their Women, Their Dispositions, Employments,
Usage by Their Husbands, Their Apparel, and Modesty.

To satisfy the curious eye of women readers, who otherwise might think their sex forgotten or not worthy a record, let them peruse these few lines wherein they may see their own happiness, if weighed in the woman's balance of these ruder Indians who scorn the tutorings of their wives or to admit them as their equals—though their qualities and industrious deservings may justly claim the preeminence and command better usage and more conjugal esteem, their persons and features being every way correspondent, their qualifications more excellent, being more loving, pitiful, and modest, mild, provident, and laborious than their lazy husbands.

Their employments be many: first their building of houses, whose frames are formed like our garden arbors, something more round, very strong and handsome, covered with close-wrought mats of their own weaving which deny entrance to any drop of rain, though it come both fierce and long, neither can the piercing north wind find a cranny through which he can convey his cooling breath.[69] They be warmer than our English houses. At the top is a square hole for the smoke's evacuation, which in rainy weather is covered with a pluver.[70] These be

68. On Indian practices of burial and mourning, see Morton, *New English Canaan,* pp. 51f.; Williams, *Key into the Language,* chap. 32; and Josselyn, *Two Voyages to New England,* p. 299. On tribes outside New England see Van der Donck, *Description of New Netherland,* pp. 86–88; Lawson, *A New Voyage,* pp. 190–193; and Heckewelder, *History, Manners, and Customs,* pp. 268–276.
69. For other accounts of New England Algonquian housing see Morton, *New English Canaan,* pp. 24–26; Williams, *Key into the Language,* chap. 6; Gookin, *Historical Collections,* pp. 9 f.; and Josselyn, *Two Voyages,* pp. 295f.
70. Not in *Oxford English Dictionary.* Wood apparently meant a rain-cover, from "pluvial": of or pertaining to rain. For a description of Indian rain-covers see Gookin, *Historical Collections,* p. 10.

such smoky dwellings that when there is good fires they are not able to stand upright, but lie all along under the smoke, never using any stools or chairs, it being as rare to see an Indian sit on a stool at home as it is strange to see an Englishman sit on his heels abroad. Their houses are smaller in the summer when their families be dispersed by reason of heat and occasions. In winter they make some fifty or threescore foot long, forty or fifty men being inmates under one roof. And as is their husbands' occasion, these poor tectonists[71] are often troubled like snails to carry their houses on their backs, sometime to fishing places, other times to hunting places, after that to a planting place where it abides the longest.

Another work is their planting of corn, wherein they exceed our English husbandmen, keeping it so clear with their clamshell hoes as if it were a garden rather than a corn field, not suffering a choking weed to advance his audacious head above their infant corn or an undermining worm to spoil his spurns. Their corn being ripe they gather it, and drying it hard in the sun convey it to their barns, which be great holes digged in the ground in form of a brass pot, sealed with rinds of trees, wherein they put their corn, covering it from the inquisitive search of their gourmandizing husbands who would eat up both their allowed portion and reserved seed if they knew where to find it. But our hogs having found a way to unhinge their barn doors and rob their garners, they are glad to implore their husbands' help to roll the bodies of trees over their holes to prevent those pioneers whose thievery they as much hate as their flesh.

Another of their employments is their summer processions to get lobsters for their husbands, wherewith they bait their hooks when they go afishing for bass or codfish. This is an everyday's walk, be the weather cold or hot, the waters rough or calm. They must dive sometimes over head and ears for a lobster, which often shakes them by their hands with a churlish nip and bids them adieu. The tide being spent, they trudge home two or three miles with a hundredweight of lobsters at their backs, and if none, a hundred scowls meet them at home and a hungry belly for two days after. Their husbands having caught any fish, they bring it in their boats as far as they can by water and there leave it; as it was their care to catch it, so it must be their wives' pains to fetch it home, or fast. Which done, they must dress it and cook it, dish it, and

71. I.e., builders or carpenters.

present it, see it eaten over their shoulders; and their loggerships[72] having filled their paunches, their sweet lullabies scramble for their scraps. In the summer these Indian women, when lobsters be in their plenty and prime, they dry them to keep for winter, erecting scaffolds in the hot sunshine, making fires likewise underneath them (by whose smoke the flies are expelled) till the substance remain hard and dry. In this manner they dry bass and other fishes without salt, cutting them very thin to dry suddenly before the flies spoil them or the rain moist them, having a special care to hang them in their smoky houses in the night and dankish weather.

In summer they gather flags,[73] of which they make mats for houses, and hemp and rushes, with dyeing stuff of which they make curious baskets with intermixed colors and protractures[74] of antic imagery. These baskets be of all sizes from a quart to a quarter,[75] in which they carry their luggage. In winter they are their husband's caterers, trudging to the clam banks for their belly timber, and their porters to lug home their venison which their laziness exposes to the wolves till they impose it upon their wives' shoulders. They likewise sew their husbands' shoes and weave coats of turkey feathers, besides all their ordinary household drudgery which daily lies upon them, so that a big belly hinders no business, nor a childbirth takes much time, but the young infant being greased and sooted,[76] wrapped in a beaver skin, bound to his good behavior with his feet up to his bum upon a board two foot long and one foot broad, his face exposed to all nipping weather, this little papoose travels about with his bare-footed mother to paddle in the icy clam banks after three or four days of age have sealed his passboard[77] and his mother's recovery.

For their carriage it is very civil, smiles being the greatest grace of their

72. A play on the word "loggerheads"—stupid, sluggardly—here used to describe Indian husbands.
73. Probably the North American cattail or similar plants.
74. I.e., drawings or designs.
75. Eight bushels; originally equal to the fourth part of a wey or load.
76. The 1634 edition reads "sooted"; in the 1635 edition the first letter is unclear and may be either a long "s" or an "f," as it is in the 1639 edition. "Sooted" seems more likely, i.e., stained dark. Thomas Morton (*New English Canaan,* p. 31) reported that infants were bathed in a stain made of walnut leaves and other dyes "to make them tawny."
77. Obsolete variant of "passport," which Wood apparently here used in a whimsical allusion to the infant's entrance into human society.

mirth; their music is lullabies to quiet their children, who generally are as quiet as if they had neither spleen or lungs. To hear one of these Indians unseen, a good ear might easily mistake their untaught voice for the warbling of a well-tuned instrument, such command have they of their voices.

These women's modesty drives them to wear more clothes than their men, having always a coat of cloth or skins wrapped like a blanket about their loins, reaching down to their hams, which they never put off in company. If a husband have a mind to sell his wife's beaver petticoat, as sometimes he doth, she will not put it off until she have another to put on. Commendable is their mild carriage and obedience to their husbands, notwithstanding all this—their [husband's] customary churlishness and savage inhumanity—not seeming to delight in frowns or offering to word it with their lords, not presuming to proclaim their female superiority to the usurping of the least title of their husband's charter, but rest themselves content under their helpless condition, counting it the woman's portion.[78]

Since the English arrival, comparison hath made them miserable, for seeing the kind usage of the English to their wives, they do as much condemn their husbands for unkindness and commend the English for their love, as their husbands—commending themselves for their wit in keeping their wives industrious—do condemn the English for their folly in spoiling good working creatures. These women resort often to the English houses, where *pares cum paribus congregatae*,[79] in sex I mean, they do somewhat ease their misery by complaining and seldom part without a relief. If her husband come to seek for his squaw and begin to bluster, the English woman betakes her to her arms, which are the warlike ladle and the scalding liquors, threatening blistering to the naked runaway, who is soon expelled by such liquid comminations.

In a word, to conclude this woman's history, their love to the English

78. Little analysis has been made of Algoquian women, but several studies explore the role and status of women in Iroquoian society. See especially Cara B. Richards, "Matriarchy or Mistake: The Role of Iroquois Women Through Time," in Verne F. Ray, ed., *Cultural Stability and Culture Change* (American Ethnological Society, *Proceedings of the 1957 Annual Spring Meeting* [Seattle, 1957]), pp. 36-45; and Judith K. Brown, "Economic Organization and the Position of Women among the Iroquois," *Ethnohistory,* 17 (1970), 151-167. On women in the Delaware tribe see Anthony F. C. Wallace, "Women, Land, and Society: Three Aspects of Aboriginal Delaware Life," *Pennsylvania Archaeologist,* 17 (1947), 1-35.

79. Transl.: "equals gathered together with equals."

hath deserved no small esteem, ever presenting them something that is either rare or desired, as strawberries, hurtleberries, raspberries, gooseberries, cherries, plums, fish, and other such gifts as their poor treasury yields them. But now it may be that this relation of the churlish and inhumane behavior of these ruder Indians towards their patient wives may confirm some in the belief of an aspersion which I have often heard men cast upon the English there, as if they should learn of the Indians to use their wives in the like manner and to bring them to the same subjection—as to sit on the lower hand and to carry water and the like drudgery. But if my own experience may out-balance an ill-grounded scandalous rumor, I do assure you, upon my credit and reputation, that there is no such matter, but the women find there as much love, respect, and ease as here in old England. I will not deny but that some poor people may carry their own water. And do not the poorer sort in England do the same, witness your London tankard bearers and your country cottagers? But this may well be known to be nothing but the rancorous venom of some that bear no good will to the plantation. For what need they carry water, seeing everyone hath a spring at his door or the sea by his house?

Thus much for the satisfaction of women, touching this entrenchment upon their prerogative, as also concerning the relation of these Indian squaws.

["A Small Nomenclator" of the Indian Language]

Because many have desired to hear some of the natives' language, I have here inserted a small nomenclator, with the names of their chief kings, rivers, months and days, whereby such as have insight into the tongues may know to what language it is most inclining; and such as desire it as an unknown language only, may reap delight, if they can get no profit.[80]

A

Aberginian—an Indian

Abamocho—the Devil

Aunum—a dog

Ausupp—a raccoon

Au so hau nouc hoc—lobster

Assawog—will you play

A saw upp—tomorrow

Ascoscoi—green

Ausomma petuc quanocke—give me some bread

Appepes naw aug—when I see it I will tell you my mind

Anno ke nugge—a sieve

An nu ocke—a bed

Autchu wompocke—today

Appause—the morn

Ascom quom pauputchim—thanks be given to God

B

Bequoquo—the head

80. Wood's version of Indian words is produced below as given in the 1635 edition, but his spelling and spacing cannot always be clearly discerned. I have consulted the 1634 and 1639 editions for clues to Wood's intentions, though in some instances the three versions are too different to allow a sure solution. For other early Indian vocabularies see the works cited in note 61 above.

Bisquant—the shoulderbones

C

Chesco kean—you lie

Commouton kean—you steal

Cram—to kill

Chickachava—*osculari podicem*[81]

Cowimms—sleeps

Cocam—the navel

Cos—the nails

Conomma—a spoon

Cossaquot—bow and arrows

Cone—the sun

Cotattup—I drink to you

Coetop—will you drink tobacco

Connucke sommona—it is almost
night

Connu—good night to you

Cowompanu sin—God morrow[82]

Coepot—ice

D

Dottaguck—the backbone

Docke taugh he necke—what is
your name

E

Et chossucke—a knife

Eat chumnis—Indian corn

Eans causuacke—four fathoms

Easu tommoc quocke—half a skin
of beaver

Epimetsis—much good may your
meat do you

F is never used

G

Gettoquaset—the great toe

Genehuncke—the forefinger

Gettoquacke—the knees

Gettoquun—the knuckles

Gettoquan—the thumb

Gegnewaw og—let me see

H

Haha—yes

Hoc—the body

Hamucke—almost

Hub hub hub—come come come

Haddo quo dunna moquonash—
where did you buy that

Haddogoe weage—who lives here

I

Isattonaneise—the bread

Icattop—faint with hunger

Icattoquam—very sleepy

K

Kean—I

Keisseanchacke—back of the hand

Ksitta—it hurts me

Kawkenog wampompeage—let me
see money

Kagmatcheu—will you eat meat

Ketottug—a whetstone

Kenie—very sharp

Kettotanese—lend me money

81. The 1634 and 1635 editions give only the Latin equivalent of the Indian word,
but the 1639 edition employs blunt Anglo-Saxon: "kisse my arsehole."
82. "God morrow" in the editions of 1634 and 1635; "good morrow" in 1639.

Kekechoi—much pain

L is not used

M
Matchet—it is naught
Mattamoi—to die
Mitchin—meat
Misquantum—very angry
Mauncheake—be gone
Matta—no
Meseig—hair
Mamanock—the eyebrees[83]
Matchanne—the nose
Mattone—the lips
Mepeiteis—the teeth
Mattickeis—the shoulders
Mettosowset—the little toe
Metosaunige—the little finger
Misquish—the veins
Mohoc—the waist
Menisowhock—the genitals
Mocossa—the black of the nail
Matchanni—very sick
Monacus—bows and arrows
Manehops—sit down
Monakinne—a coat
Mawcus sinnus—a pair of shoes
Matchemauquot—it stinketh
Muskanai—a bone
Menota—a basket
Meatchis—be merry
Mawpaw—it snows
Mawnaucoi—very strong
Mutcheou—a very poor man
Monosketenog—what's this

Mouskett—the breech
Matchet wequon—very blunt
Matta ka tau caushana—will you
     not trade
Mowhacheis—Indian gold

N
Nancompees—a boy
Nickesquaw—a maid
Nean—you
Nippe—water
Nasamp—pottage
Nota—six
Nisquan—the elbow
Noenaset—the third toe
Nahenan—a turkey
Niccone—a blackbird
Naw naunidge—the middle finger
Napet—the arm
Nitchicke—the hand
Notoquap—the skin
Nogcus—the heart
Nobpaw nocke—the breastbone
Nequaw—the thighs
Netop—a friend
Nonmia—give me
Noeicantop—how do you
Nawhaw nissis—farewell
Noei pauketan—by and by kill
Nenetah ha—I'll fight with you
Noei comquocke—a codfish
Nepaupe—stand by
No ottut—a great journey
Necautauh hau—no such matter
Noewamma—he laugheth
Noeshow—a father

83. Obsolete form of "eyebrows."

Nitka—a mother
Netchaw—a brother
Notonquous—a kinsman
Nenomous—a kinswoman
Nau mau nais—my son
Taunais [sic]—my daughter
No einshom—give me corn
Nemnis—take it
Nenimma nequitta ta auchu—give me a span of anything .
Nees nis ca su acke—two fathom
Notchumoi—a little strong
Negacawgh hi—lend me
Nebuks quam—adieu
Noe winyah—come in
Naut seam—much weary
Noe wammaw ause—I love you
Net noe whaw missu—a man of a middle stature

O
Ottucke—a deer
Occone—a deerskin
Oquan—the heel
Ottump—a bow
Ottommaocke—tobacco
Ottannapeake—the chin
Occotucke—the throat
Occasu—half a quarter
Unquagh [sic] saw au—you are cunning
Ontoquos—a wolf

P
Pow-wow—a conjurer or wizard
Petta sinna—give me a pipe of tobacco
Pooke—colt's foot
Pappouse—a child

Petucquanocke—bread
Picke—a pipe
Ponesanto—make a fire
Papowne—winter
Pequas—a fox
Pausochu—a little journey
Peamissin—a little
Peacumshis—work hard
Pokitta—smoke
Petogge—a bag
Paucasn—a quarter
Pausawniscosu—half a fathom
Peunctaumocke—much pray
Pesissu—a little man
Pausepissoi—the sun is rising
Pouckshaa—it is broken
Poebugketaas—you burn
Poussu—a big-bellied woman

Q
Quequas nummos—what cheer
Quequas nim—it is almost day
Quog quosh—make haste
Quenobpuuncke—a stool
Quenops—be quiet

R is never used

S
Sagamore—a king
Sachem—idem
Sannup—a man
Squaw—a woman
Squitta—a fire spark
Suggig—a bass
Seasicke—a rattlesnake
Shannucke—a squirrel
Skesicos—the eyes

Sickeubecke—the neck

Supskinge—the wrist bones

Socottocanus—the breastbone

Squehincke—blood

Siccaw quant—the hams

Sis sau causke—the shins

Suppiske—ankle bones

Seat—the foot

Seaseap—a duck

Suckis suacke—a clam

Sequan—the summer

Soekepup—he will bite

Sis—come out

Squi—red

Swanscaw suacko—three fathoms

Sawawampeage—very weak

Succomme—I will eat you

Sasketupe—a great man

T

Taubut ne an hee—thanks heartily

Tantacum—beat him

Tap in—go in

Titta—I cannot tell

Tahanyah—what news

Tonagus—the ears

Tannicke—a cranny

Thaw—the calf of the leg

Tahaseat—the sole of the foot

Tasseche quonunck—the instep

Tonokete naum—whither go you

Tannissin may—which is the way

Tunketappin—where live you

Tonocco wam—where have you been

Tasis— a pair of stockings

Tockucke—a hatchet

Towwow—a sister

Tom maushew—a husband

Tookesin—enough sleep

Titto kean I catoquam—do you nod and sleep

Tau kequam—very heavy

Tauh coi—it is very cold

V [interchangeable with "U"]

Vkepemanous—the breastbone

Unkesheto—will you truck

W

Wampompeage—Indian money

Winnet—very good

Web—a wife

Wigwam—a house

Wawmott—enough

Whenan—the tongue

Whauksis—a fox

Wawpatucke—a goose

Wawpiske—the belly

Whoe nuncke—a ditch

Wappinne—the wind

Wawtom—understand you

Wompey—white

Wa aoy—the sun is down

Waacoh—the day breaks

Wekemawquot—it smells sweet

Weneikinne—it is very handsome

Whissu hochuck—the kettle boileth

Waawnew—you have lost your way

Woenaunta—it is a warm summer

Wompoca—tomorrow

Wawmauseu—an honest man

Weneicu—a rich man

Weitagcone—a clear day

Wawnauco—yesterday

X [is] never used

Y

Yeips—sit down

Yaus—the sides
Yaugh—there
Yough yough—now
Yoakes—lice

The number of 20.

A quit	1	Ocqinta	6	Apponna quit	11	Apponaquinta	16
Nees	2	Enotta	7	Apponees	12	Apponenotta	17
Nis	3	Sonaske	8	Apponis	13	Apponsonaske	18
Yoaw	4	Assaquoquin	9	Appoyoaw	14	Apponasquoquin	19
Abbona	5	Piocke	10	Apponabonna	15	Neenisschicke	20

The Indians count their time by nights and not by days, as followeth.

Sawup, 1 sleeps
Isoqunnocquock, 2 sleeps
Sucqunnocquocke, 3 sleeps
Yoawqunnocquock, 4 sleeps
Abonetta ta
  sucqunnocquock, 5 sleeps
Nequitta ta sucqunnocquock,
  6 sleeps

Enotta ta
  sucqunnocquock, 7 sleeps
Soesicta.
  sucqunnocquock, 8 sleeps
Pausa quoquin
  sucqunnocquock, 9 sleeps
Pawquo
  qunnocquock, 10 sleeps

How they call their months.

A quit-appause, 1 months
Nees-appause, 2 months
Nis-appause, 3 months
Yoaw appause, 4 months
Abonna appause, 5 months
Nequit appause, 6 months
Enotta appause, 7 months
Sonaske appause, 8 months
Assaquoquin appause, 9 months
Piocke appause, 10 months

Appona quit appause, 11 months
Appon nees appause, 12 months
Appon nis appause, 13 months
Appon yoaw appause, 14 months
Nap nappona appause, 15 months
Nap napocquint appause,
  16 months
Nap nap enotta appause,
  17 months
Napsoe sicke appause, 18 months

Nappawsoquoquin appause, 19 months

Neesnischicke appause, 20 months

Neesnischicke appon a quit appause, 21 months

Neesnischick apponees

appause, 22 months

Neesnischick apponis appause, 23 months

Neesnischick appo yoaw appause, 24 months

The names of the Indians as they be divided into several countries.

| Tarrenteens | Aberginians | Pequants | Connectacuts |
| Churchers | Narragansets | Nipnets | Mowhacks |

The names of Sagamores.

Woenohaquahham—Anglice King John

Montowompate—Anglice King James

Mausquonomend—Igowam saga-more

Chickkatawbut—Naponset saga-more

Nepawhamis, Nannoponnacund, Asteco, Nattonanite, Assotomo-wite, Noenotchuock

Nassawwhonan, Woesemagen— Two sagamores of Nipust

Canonicus—Narragansett sagamore

Osomeagen—Sagamore of the Pequants [Pequots]

Kekut—Petchutacut sagamore

Pissacannua—A sagamore and most noted necromancer

Sagamores to the East and North-east bearing rule amongst the Churchers and Tarrenteens

The names of the most noted habitations.

Merrimack	Swampscot
Igowam	Nahant
Igoshaum	Winnisimmet
Chobocco *Anglice*[84]	Mishaum
Nahumkeake—Salem	Mishaumut—Charlestown
Saugus	Massachusetts—Boston

84. I.e., English. Below that word Wood gives the English place names of several Indian locations. All Indian names are here given as Wood spelled them, but most place names now have slightly different orthography.

Mistick

Pigsgusset—Watertown

Naponset

Matampan—Dorchester

Pawtuxet—Plymouth

Wessaguscus

Conihosset

Mannimeed

Soewampset

Situate

Amuskeage

Pemmiquid

Saketehoc

Piscataqua

Cannibek

Penopscot

Pantoquid

Nawquot

Musketoquid

Nipnet

Whawcheusets

At what places be rivers of note.[85]

Cannibeck River

Merrimacke River

Tchobocco River

Saugus River

Mistick River

Mishaum River

Naponset River

Wessaguscus River

Luddams Ford

Narragansets River

Musketoquid River

Hunniborne River

Connectacut River

Finis

85. Most of the rivers listed by Wood still retain their Indian names, though often with minor alterations in spelling. Luddam's Ford and Hunniborne River were named for early settlers. On Luddam see *Winthrop's Journal*, 1, 94 .

Selected Readings

The following writings shed further light on William Wood's varied interests, especially early settlement, natural history, and the Indians.

SEVENTEENTH CENTURY WORKS

Bradford, William. *History of Plymouth Plantation.* Edited by Worthington C. Ford. 2 vols. Boston, 1912

[Bradford, William, and Winslow, Edward]. *A Relation or Journal of the English Plantation Settled at Plymouth in New England. . . . .* Edited by Dwight B. Heath as *A Journal of the Pilgrims at Plymouth.* New York, 1963.

Child, Robert, to Samuel Hartlib, 24 Dec. 1645, in Colonial Society of Massachusetts, *Publications,* XXXVIII (*Transactions, 1947-51*), 50-53.

Eliot, John. *A Brief Narrative of the Progress of the Gospel Among the Indians of New England, 1670.* Boston, 1868.

Eliot, John. "John Eliot's Description of New England in 1650," Massachusetts Historical Society, *Proceedings,* 2 ser. II (1885-1886), 44-50.

Gookin, Daniel. *Historical Collections of the Indians in New England.* Boston, 1792; repr. New York, 1972.

Gorges, Fernando. "Brief Narration of the Original Undertakings of the Advancement of Plantations into the Parts of America. . . ," in Maine Historical Society, *Collections*, 1 ser. II (1847), 1–65 (2nd pagination).

[Gorges, Fernando]. "A Brief Relation of the Discovery and Plantation of New England," in Massachusetts Historical Society, *Collections*, 2 ser. IX (1823), 1–25.

Higginson, Francis. *New-Englands Plantation*. Salem, Mass., 1908.

Hubbard, William. *A General History of New England*. (Massachusetts Historical Society, *Collections*, 2 ser. V–VI.) Boston, 1815.

Hubbard, William. *A Narrative of the Troubles with the Indians in New-England, from the First Planting Thereof to the Present Time*. Edited by Samuel G. Drake as *The History of the Indian Wars in New England. . . .* 2 vols. Rosbury, Mass., 1865.

Hutchinson, Thomas, ed. *Hutchinson Papers*. (The Prince Society, *Publications*, II–IV.) Albany, 1865.

James, Sydney V., Jr., ed. *Three Visitors to Early Plymouth: Letters about the Pilgrims. . . .* Plymouth, Mass., 1963.

Johnson, Edward. *Johnson's Wonder-Working Providence, 1628–1651*. Edited by J. Franklin Jameson. New York, 1910.

Josselyn, John. *An Account of Two Voyages to New England*, in Massachusetts Historical Society, *Collections*, 3 ser. III (1833), 211–354.

Josselyn, John. *New-Englands Rarities Discovered*, in American Antiquarian Society, *Transactions and Collections*, IV (1860), 130–238.

Lechford, Thomas. *Plain Dealing: or, News from New England*. New York, 1867; repr. New York, 1969.

Mather, Increase. *A Relation of the Troubles which have hapned in New-England By reason of the Indians there. From the Year 1614 to the Year 1675*. Edited by Samuel G. Drake as *Early History of New England*. Boston, 1864.

Maverick, Samuel. "A Briefe Description of New England and the Severall Townes therein, together with the Present government thereof." Massachusetts Historical Society, *Proceedings*, 2 ser. I (1884–85), 231–249.

Megapolensis, Johannes. "A Short Account of the Mohawk Indians. . . ." in J. Franklin Jameson, ed. *Narratives of New Netherland, 1609–1664*. New York, 1909.

Morton, Thomas. *New English Canaan, or New Canaan.* Amsterdam, 1637; repr. New York, 1972.

New England's First Fruits: with Divers other Special Matters Concerning that Country. New York, 1865. Also reprinted in Samuel Eliot Morison, *The Founding of Harvard College* (Boston, 1935), pp. 419–447.

Records of the Court of Assistants of the Colony of the Massachusetts Bay, 1630–1692. 3 vols. Boston, 1901–1908.

Shurtleff, Nathaniel E., ed. *Records of the Governor and Company of the Massachusetts Bay in New England.* 5 vols. Boston, 1853–54.

Shurtleff, Nathaniel E., and Pulsifer, David, eds. *Records of the Colony of New Plymouth.* 12 vols. Boston, 1855–1861.

Smith, John. *Travels and Works of Captain John Smith.* Edited by Edward Arber and A. G. Bradley. 2 vols. Edinburgh, 1910.

White, John. *The Planter's Plea, or the Grounds of Plantations Examined, and usuall Objectives Answered.* London, 1630; repr. Rockport, Mass., 1930.

Williams, Roger. *A Key into the Language of America.* Edited by John J. Teunissen and Evelyn J. Hinz. Detroit, 1973.

Winslow, Edward. "Good Newes from New England," in Edward Arber, ed. *The Story of the Pilgrim Fathers.* London, 1897.

Winthrop, John. *Winthrop's Journal, "History of New England," 1630–1649.* Edited by James Kendall Hosmer. 2 vols. New York, 1908.

Winthrop Papers. Edited by the Massachusetts Historical Society. 5 vols. Boston, 1929–1947.

Young, Alexander, ed. *Chronicles of the First Planters of the Colony of Massachusetts Bay, from 1623 to 1636.* Boston, 1846; repr. New York, 1970.

Young, Alexander, ed. *Chronicles of the Pilgrim Fathers of the Colony of Plymouth, from 1602 to 1625.* Boston, 1841; repr. New York, 1971.

MODERN STUDIES

Adams, Charles Francis. *Three Episodes in Massachusetts History.* 2 vols. Boston, 1896.

Adams, James Truslow. *The Founding of New England.* Boston, 1921.

DeForest, John W. *History of the Indians of Connecticut.* Hartford, 1852.

Flannery, Regina. *An Analysis of Coastal Algonquian Culture.* Washington, D. C., 1939.

Hodge, Frederick Webb, ed. *Handbook of American Indians North of Mexico.* 2 vols. Washington, D. C., 1907.

Jennings, Francis. *The Invasion of America: Indians, Colonialism, and the Cant of Conquest.* Chapel Hill, N. C., 1975.

Kellaway, William. *The New England Company, 1649–1776.* New York, 1962.

Leach, Douglas Edwards. *The Northern Colonial Frontier, 1607–1763.* New York, 1966.

Morison, Samuel Eliot. *Builders of the Bay Colony.* Boston, 1930.

Palfrey, John Gorham. *History of New England.* 5 vols. Boston, 1865–1890.

Pilling, James C. *Bibliography of the Algonquian Languages.* Washington, D. C., 1891.

Rutman, Darrett B. *Husbandmen of Plymouth: Farms and Villages in the Old Colony, 1620–1692.* Boston, 1967.

Rutman, Darrett B. *Winthrop's Boston: Portrait of a Puritan Town.* Chapel Hill, N. C., 1965.

Savage, James. *A Genealogical Dictionary of the First Settlers of New England. . . .* 4 vols. Boston, 1860.

Swanton, John R. *The Indian Tribes of North America.* Washington, D. C., 1952.

Speck, Frank G. *Territorial Subdivisions and Boundaries of the Wampanoag, Massachusetts, and Nauset Indians.* New York, 1928.

Vaughan, Alden T. *New England Frontier: Puritans and Indians, 1620–1675.* Boston, 1965.

Weeden, William B. *Economic and Social History of New England, 1620–1789.* 2 vols. Boston, 1890.

Willoughby, Charles C. *Antiquities of the New England Indians.* Cambridge, Mass., 1935.

INDEX

Library of Congress Cataloging in Publication Data

Wood, William, fl. 1629–1635.
  New England's prospect.

  (The Commonwealth series)
  "Based on Wood's second edition (1635)."
  Bibliography: p.
  Includes index.
  1. Massachusetts—Description and travel. 2. Massa-
chusetts—History—Colonial period, ca. 1600–1775.
3. Indians of North America—Massachusetts. 4. Massa-
chusetts, language—Glossaries, vocabularies, etc.
I. Vaughan, Alden T., 1929— II. Title. III. Series:
The Commonwealth series (Amherst, Mass.)
F67.W877 1977   974.4'02   76-45051
ISBN 0-87023-226-6